Peter Scothern

New Wine Press

New Wine Press
P.O. Box 17
Chichester, PO20 6YB
England

Bible quotations are from the Authorised Version.

Scothern, Peter
    Miracles.
    1. Christian church. Ministry of healing
    I. Title
    265.82

ISBN 0 947852 64 6

Typeset by Alpha Typesetting and Graphic Design Ltd
17 New Road, Chatham, Kent
Printed in England by Clays Ltd, St Ives plc

Contents

Preface

It is now over forty years since teenager Peter Scothern collapsed with a serious illness and was confined to bed for many weeks. There were times when he felt that his very life was slipping away. One day, feeling greatly depressed and low in spirit he turned to the Bible for comfort and consolation. The Holy Spirit miraculously illuminated the scriptures and young Peter called upon Christ for salvation. The living Saviour entered his heart and completely changed his life. His conversion was amazing, resulting in an entirely new way of life.

Faith Came Alive

Peter Scothern's wiltering faith suddenly burst into a new dynamic force. Shortly after his conversion, Peter Scothern again consulted the scriptures for Divine Healing. As he opened the family Bible at random, imagine his surprise when he immediately read:

"IS ANY SICK AMONG YOU? LET HIM CALL FOR THE ELDERS OF THE CHURCH, AND LET THEM PRAY OVER HIM, ANOINTING HIM WITH OIL IN THE NAME OF THE LORD JESUS, AND THE PRAYER OF FAITH *SHALL* SAVE THE SICK, AND THE LORD *SHALL* RAISE HIM UP; AND IF HE HAS COMMITTED SINS THEY *SHALL* BE FORGIVEN HIM." (James 5:14 & 15).

Peter promptly obeyed these Divine instructions. The elders attended and faithfully anointed him with oil in the name of the Lord.

The prayer of faith brought down the power of God and he was electrified by the Lord's healing grace for a full thirty minutes. He promptly rose up from his sick bed and was MIRACULOUSLY MADE WHOLE. From that hour Peter has faithfully preached, ministered and declared God's double grace to all – "THE SALVATION

OF THE SOUL AND THE DIVINE HEALING OF MIND AND BODY."

It is his forthright declaration of these TWIN NEW TESTAMENT MINISTRIES that has resulted in numerous miracles of grace and healing worldwide. Tens of thousands have gathered to hear this humble and yet powerful servant of God proclaim the emancipating gospel of Christ. Hundreds of deaf have been made to hear, the lame to walk and the blind to see just like Bible days.

The BBC televised a remarkable documentary entitled "THE KILGETTY HEALER," to highlight Evangelist Peter Scothern's outstanding ministry of Divine Healing. For over forty years this dedicated international healing minister has been effectively used by the power of Christ in the healing of the infirm, oppressed, afflicted, incurable and fearful

Although the ministry of the gospel confirmed by Divine miracles is now much more accepted, it has required a pioneer work over the years. Peter Scothern has been used by God in this ministry, visiting numerous countries and seeing the hand of the Lord at work.

He has ministered in all denominations and has been involved in community revivals in West Wales, the Midlands and Essex. Abroad he has visited the U.S.A., Europe, Africa and India where over 75,000 have attended his outdoor miracle crusades.

Thousands have come to Christ through his simple but powerful gospel ministry, and he has witnessed hundreds of miracles of healing – the deaf, dumb, blind, lame, cancer victims and every sort of sickness.

This book is intended to inspire your faith to believe and receive from the Lord the things thought impossible until now. May the Lord speak to you through it.

1

The Beginning of Miracles

I will let my story unfold from the time when I was but six years of age. I always loved gardens. My grandfather enjoyed my company as he tended his vegetables and fruit trees.

One day I was day-dreaming when I chanced to see a strange glow coming from a small hollybush. I went over to the bush, and stood looking at it. Suddenly a voice came from the tree and although I failed to understand what was said I fully realised that the voice was addressed to me. In a state of shock being fearful of this unusual development I turned tail and ran back home.

I was always to remember this unforgettable experience and believed it to be my very first encounter with God.

A Childhood Miracle

One of my childhood treasures was a magnifying glass from which I obtained endless pleasure. One day I mislaid it and after a fruitless search thought it was really lost. In desperation I fell to my knees and prayed earnestly for God to help me. Hastily I shouted, "Come on Lord, please help me find it! You must know where it is, please help me find it!"

This was a strange way to approach the Almighty God and yet my prayer was trustful and sincere. I was ashamed afterwards when God faithfully responded. Rising from my knees I glanced out of the window and promptly perceived something flashing in the grass below. Carefully noting the spot, I raced down to the garden and sure enough, there was the coveted magnifying glass. Returning to my room once again I fell on my knees saying, "Thank you Lord. A big thank you! and by the way God, I am sorry I was so rude just now." Our merciful God is so understanding at times like these.

One thing becomes clear at this point. I was beginning to pray to God as a natural course and God graciously responded to encourage my faith.

Problems Within

As I approached my teenage years my spiritual growth was greatly hindered by the tendency to lose my temper accompanied by a developing jealous disposition. For some period this state of affairs undermined my confidence and sapped my spiritual desires. I realised I was fighting a losing battle and subsequently turned my attention to secular success.

When I left school, it was with a record for hard work, having passed all my exams, some with honours. I continued to attend a local church occasionally still hoping for a solution to my spiritual problems. However, the more I struggled with my besetting weaknesses the deeper I fell into despair having yet to realise that only the power of Christ could effect a lasting victory in my soul.

Later I followed my father in work, having obtained a clerkship in the Metal Box Company where, after a year I was promoted to foreman in the Component Stores at the young age of 16 years.

I was blessed with an excellent memory which later enabled me to memorize whole passages from the Bible, but I remained an inwardly disturbed person still labouring under the conviction of sin. At the age of seventeen years, however, God dramatically answered my heartcry and blessed me with a vision of the crucified Jesus. This vision made a lasting impact upon my life. I surrendered my life to Jesus Christ and was immediately transformed. I was "born again" – old habits passed away and all things became new. I began to experience the wonder of the Christian life and the companionship of the Lord Jesus Christ.

A Personal Healing Miracle

Some time prior to my conversion however, my health had started to deteriorate, agitated by my spiritual restlessness and searching for peace. My nerves were in a poor state and one day I collapsed and was confined to bed for some weeks. The local doctor seemed rather puzzled by my condition and ordered complete rest. Later he advised a specialist to call. Just prior to this visit another miracle occurred. I was resting in bed, feeling very low and depressed. At times it seemed as if my very life was slipping away and yet there burned in my heart a sincere desire to serve the Lord. So I fervently prayed and once again my heartcry was answered in a most remarkable way. I took up the family Bible and opened the pages at random.

Imagine my surprise and amazement when I immediately read,

"Is any sick among you? Let him call for the elders of the Church, and let them pray over him, anointing him with oil in the name of the Lord: and the prayer of faith shall save the sick, and the Lord shall raise him up; and if he has committed sins they shall be forgiven him."

(James 5:14,15)

I promptly acted upon the Lord's instructions. The elders attended and anointed me in the name of Jesus. The prayer of faith brought down the power of God and I was electrified by the healing grace for a full thirty minutes. I immediately rose from my sick bed perfectly whole and praising the Lord! This remarkable experience stimulated a burning desire to make a study of the New Testament healing ministry.

The Twofold Ministry

From that hour, whenever I was given an opportunity to preach the gospel I never hesitated to make known the double work of grace, i.e. the salvation of the soul and the divine healing of the body. It was this two fold biblical truth that was to provide the basis for my worldwide ministry.

I have constantly affirmed that the gospel came not in word only but also in deed and power. Jesus never sent His disciples just to preach. He also commanded them to heal the sick, cleanse the leper, raise the dead and cast out demons. The gospel of the kingdom must be presented with divine confirmation, supernatural proof and heaven sent evidence. This New Testament truth is one of the foundation pillars of my God-given ministry. I cannot separate the preaching of the gospel from the ministry of healing and deliverance, they must go hand in hand just like New Testament days.

The Hilda Miller Miracle

One of the first miracles of healing occurred during my ministry in Croydon. I first set eyes on Hilda Miller when she occupied a front seat at one of those powerful services. She was very conspicuous wearing a special headgear and neck support which partly covered her face.

Her body was imprisoned in a huge surgical contraption with leg plasters strapped to her limbs. She had lived in this restrictive cage day and night for many wearying years. I was moved with compassion and stepped from the platform to question her.

She believed the Lord could make her whole and was quite willing to surrender to Christ.

I gently took her by the hand and led her to the front of the assembled company. Acquainting all present with the facts of her case, I invited the congregation to join in believing prayer. Immediately the power of the Lord fell upon Hilda and she was completely radiant.

She began blessing and praising God declaring that she was miraculously cured. One of the lady counsellors escorted her into a private room where sixty-nine years old Hilda removed her surgical contraptions and appliances. She returned to the service completely healed, and began jumping, bending and running around glorifying God. The congregation responded with joy and excitement. She waved her surgical jacket and legplasters to the delight of all present. The entire assembly rose up worshipping and praising God. Two years later Hilda Miller, at the age of seventy one years, was married. She lived a very active life attending her garden and assisting with the home decorating. She travelled many miles testifying of Christ's triumphant miracle in her life. Her many discarded surgical contraptions were frequently displayed as evidence of this mighty work of grace. God faithfully witnessed to the twofold New Testament ministry of salvation for the soul and body.

A Living Voice From Heaven

I constantly consult the scriptures for inspiration and guidance, almost like a child asking for father's direction. When I was in need of a vehicle for the Lord's ministry I visited a local car showroom where

I was attracted to a small van which I felt would adequately suit my purpose. Returning home I told the Lord about the matter. Placing the Bible on the table I sought special guidance from the word of truth.

Prayerfully opening the Bible, my eyes fastened upon a most appropriate scripture. *"Go near, and join thyself to this chariot"* (Acts 8:29). The instruction, though somewhat amusing, certainly reassured me to proceed with the purchase of the van. The Lord subsequently met my every need.

Some years later, when I required premises for an office, I had further reason to seek the Lord's direction. Again after prayerful consultation, imagine my joyful surprise when upon opening the scriptures I read, *"I have prepared the house, and room for the camels"*, (Genesis 24:31). The camels, of course, were the faithful staff who have strenuously laboured with me over many years.

To me the Word of God is a living voice from heaven. When I open the Bible Jesus steps from the pages. I read the scriptures slowly and deliberately as if Jesus Himself is at my side quoting His own word.

The Word of God is a present tense living voice from above! "God's Word is God's Will. God's Word is a light unto my feet and a lamp unto my path. It is more than a historical record. It is the very Word of the Almighty speaking to me NOW!"

So the anointed, ever present WORD feeds my spirit and from its pages emanates Divine counsel, wisdom, life and power. The living word is the strength of my faith and the inspiration of my believing.

A God Imparted Faith

During the memorable Indian crusades I faced a spiritual crisis. As I stepped to the platform and saw tens of thousands of souls in darkness and hundreds of sick and suffering laid out before me my faith wavered and weakened. I wanted to run away and hide. In the silence of my soul I was engaged in a spiritual conflict such as I had never previously experienced. I tried all the usual practices to boost my sagging confidence but I was even more demoralised. In desperation I turned once again to the Word of God and my eyes fell upon a most revealing verse of scripture.

"I am crucified with Christ: nevertheless I live: yet not I, but Christ liveth in me: and the life which I now live in the flesh I live by the faith of the Son of God, who loved me, and gave Himself for me."

(Galatians 2:20)

The scales fell from my doubting heart and I saw clearly that I must live BY THE FAITH OF THE SON OF GOD and not my own believing. I cast away my wavering faith and opened my doubting heart to the very faith of Jesus Christ, and Son of God. A new heaven-born confidence filled my being. I knew from the moment that demoralising doubt was a thing of the past. I now believed for all things Jesus promised.

The first dynamic effect of this faith revolution occurred when I was reading the scriptures. I quoted the Word of God with such faith and authority, that upon publicly reading the Bible story of the healing of the blind man, when Jesus said, "Receive thy sight!" – a blind woman in the vast assembly suddenly received her sight. She was thrust to the platform by excited friends declaring that her sight was restored at the precise moment I said, "Receive thy sight". So the WORD of healing quoted two thousand years ago by Jesus the Son of God suddenly worked today. "Yes, the Word of the Lord is a creative force feeding my faith and producing miracles as I speak under the powerful anointing God and in the peerless name of Jesus."

Hearing the Voice of The Lord

During one of my recent crusade services a gentleman came forward for divine healing. I had never previously set eyes upon him. He was a complete stranger – and yet as I conversed with him I was able to give him a complete history of his problem and then prescribe the divine remedy.

It was this operation of the "word of knowledge" which convinced him beyond doubt of my God given ministry.

Sometimes the operation of this gift enables me to perceive the hidden needs of members of the congregation. This divine revelation encourages those present to trust Jesus with their special problems. I recall one such incident when the Holy Spirit impressed upon me the undisclosed need of a distressed mother greatly burdened for her teenage daughter. I was enabled by the the Holy Spirit to describe the problem in perfect detail. The anxious mother, recognising the divine revelation, promptly stood to her feet and proclaimed, "I am the mother, please pray for my daughter."

On another occasion I was questioned by a respectable Christian as to why he had not been divinely healed from his arthritic condition. The sufferer was astonished when I informed him that his problem was related to a debt which he had refused to pay. Without further question the sick man produced his cheque book, completed the slip and then signed it. Within moments the Lord's power fell upon him and he was released from his affliction.

Remarkable Dream Revelation

Divine revelation occasionally comes to me by the means of dreams. God grants sometimes a dramatic insight into coming events through this gift. Prior to the "Tube Train Disaster" in London I dreamt that I was travelling as a passenger in a tube train which crashed. I told my staff of this remarkable dream a few days before it occurred. I was convinced the Lord had granted me this revelation so that I could intercede for the victims. When the complete details of the tragedy were made known they tallied exactly with those revealed in the dream. One lady trapped in the wreckage was heard TO CALL upon the Name of Jesus to be saved.

Prior to a serious earthquake in China which claimed tens of thousands of lives I had a vivid dream of an industrial city being destroyed by severe earth tremors. I visualised factories collapsing and falling into the bowels of the earth; tall buildings sliding into destruction and a whole city totally devastated. This dream vision was so disturbing that sleep left me during the rest of the night and so I spent those early hours praying for the victims of the catastrophe.

A Voice from Heaven

En route to West Wales I was travelling along the M5 motorway following two slow moving vehicles. As I was contemplating overtaking, a voice as clear as any human voice said, "Do not overtake!" I was startled by this sudden intrusion, and unhesitantly obeyed. A minute or so later, a fast car travelling in the opposite direction, swerved across the central reservation and crashed into the first vehicle which burst into flames. The second vehicle took the full impact and exploded into fragments. The debris from the shattered vehicles rained down upon my car as I braked to a halt. The motorway was blanketed with black smoke. I offered a hurried prayer for the Lord's strength and hastened to help. The accident victims were in a terrible state as they lay motionless on the motorway. With God given confidence I laid hands on two of them offering prayer for new life in the name of Jesus. Both victims began breathing freely as I fervently prayed. I witnessed the risen life of Jesus quickening their mortal bodies. Then I encourged them to call upon the Lord for salvation and comfort.

Soon the ambulances rushed them away to hospital. Later I learned that both accident victims were alive and well and giving praise to God.

I am fully convinced that the voice from heaven had forewarned and preserved me in a most miraculous manner.

2
Miracles of Jesus

Wherever Jesus went there were miracles. Miracles of grace, miracles of healing, miracles of deliverance, miracles and more miracles. Jesus came from the realm of miracles. His conception was a miracle, His birth was a miracle, His life and death were miracles.

The person of the Holy Spirit overshadowed the Virgin Mary and placed in her womb the seed of the Christ Child. Her conception was a miracle of God. Mary was with child BY THE HOLY GHOST. Jesus was not conceived after the natural order but after the supernatural – the miraculous order. Jesus was a miracle baby. For nine months Mary carried a miracle child in her womb. Wonder of wonders.

Some forty years ago I repented of my sins and invited the living Christ into my heart. Jesus came into my life, I received the same Jesus who was born of Mary. The very same Christ entered the womb of my spirit. I was born again – not of corruptible seed but of incorruptible seed which is the Word of God. Within my life is a new miracle nature – the Jesus nature. Old things have passed away and ALL THINGS have become new. I am a new Creation – a new Creature. Jesus was conceived in my heart by the Holy Ghost the very moment I was "born again".

I was reborn from above. A new man – a Jesus man. This is the outstanding miracle of the Christian life.

God wants to change us all from the inside. So called modern Christian philosophies want to change us from the outside. The Lord is concerned about the heart. He wants to change us from the inside.

Sea of Galilee Miracle

Luke details the phenomenal incident of how Jesus miraculously calmed the turbulent waters of Galilee. With just three authoritative words, "PEACE BE STILL." Jesus stilled the raging storm, to the amazement of His disciples. Little wonder they said one to another,

> *"What manner of man is this, for He commandeth even the winds, and they obey him?"*

> (Matthew 8:25)

From 1952 it has been my regular privilege to visit the Holy Land, during which I have experienced a number of memorable visitations from the Lord.

I remember taking a group of Christian folk on a boat trip across the Sea of Galilee. We were scheduled to hold a short service in the middle of the sea. Sailing from Tiberias the waters were calm and tranquil. We had not travelled very far however when a fierce wind began churning the sea. The boat started rocking violently from side to side. It seemed our mid lake service would have to be cancelled.

The Holy Spirit suddenly brought to mind the incident in Luke 8 and I proposed to my Christian group that they lift up their hands in Jesus name. They cried out in unison, "PEACE BE STILL!, **PEACE BE STILL!**." The command rang out loud and clear and God's presence was powerfully experienced. Within seconds the rocking ceased and the waters calmed.

Everyone present was ecstatic with joy and began praising the name of the Lord. We then enjoyed a most blessed service upon the still waters of Galilee.

Convention Tent Miracle

During one of our West Wales conventions under the "big tent" we experienced a similar miracle. A violent storm hit the coast of West Wales demolishing a Butlins Camp causing thousands of pounds worth of damage. The same devastating wind struck our convention site that evening.

The huge tent supports shook violently. The canvas billowed and strained at its moorings. It was too dangerous to hold the service under such circumstances. It was suggested that we transfer the meeting to the nearby church.

Again the Holy Spirit brought to my remembrance the Luke 8 incident. I retraced my steps and asked the brethren to raise their hands and repeat in the Lord's name "PEACE BE STILL!, PEACE BE STILL!."

This authoritative command had the same effect. The boisterous wind promptly subsided and the convention tent gradually settled down. Throughout the evening there was hardly a breath of wind. Everyone was pleasantly surprised and gave united praise and glory to Jesus for such an unprecedented happening.

Miracle of Divine Protection

During one of my recent pilgrimages to the Holy Land my group visited the ancient town of Bethlehem. Protesting Arab youths were involved in the stoning of the cars and coaches. The night previous to the visit the Lord warned me in a dream of trouble ahead. The dream showed that my group of twenty-five Christian folk would be divided into two groups.

Suddenly there was a loud bang, as if a plate glass window had violently exploded. As this occurred in between the two separated groups no one was hurt, and I was not greatly disturbed. When I awoke from the dream I pondered a long time on its meaning.

Next morning our visit to Bethlehem passed without incident. The town was comparatively quiet due to a strike that had closed all the local Arab shops and stores. Upon returning to Jerusalem, however, the passengers on the coach sat in two groups – one at the rear of the coach – the other at the front – as depicted in the dream. Suddenly there was a resounding bang, as one of the central windows of the coach exploded into a thousand pieces. A fair size stone lay under the shattered window. The suddenness of the event startled everyone. Only minutes previously two young passengers seated near the point of impact had moved to the rear of the coach. Miracle of miracles no one was hurt or injured. The warning dream had clearly served its purpose and we joined in praising and glorifying God for our miraculous deliverance.

God Chooses Time and Place

Divine miracles are a demonstration of God's sovereign power and glory. He alone chooses the time and place.

Peter and John were journeying to the temple when they healed a man who was lame from his mother's womb. I wonder how many times Jesus may have passed the same man without curing him? Yes, God chooses the time and place and the channels through whom He wills His miracle working power.

Poisoned Food Miracle

During my missionary trek into Calabar West Africa, I was constantly protected by the Lord.

Staying overnight in a village schoolroom I was invited, along with my missionary companion to an evening meal. There was much hostility at that time towards the "white preachers" and I did not realise that the local witch doctor had poisoned our food. As we sat down to eat, a divine voice whispered, "TOUCH NOT THE UNCLEAN THING! TOUCH NOT THE UNCLEAN THING!"

I was greatly puzzled by this warning and told my fellow minister. We decided to throw a portion of the food to a hungry bush dog begging outside. To our astonishment the poor creature simply rolled over and died having eagerly devoured the poisoned meat. Both our lives were miraculously preserved by God's "still small voice".

Jesus can turn the vilest sinners into true Sons of the Living God.

Since the early 1970's I have been committed to an itinerant ministry. London, Bath, Hereford, Birmingham, Leicester, Leeds, Weston, West Wales, Cornwall, have been included in my regular schedule. Summer conventions have also been held at Eastbourne, Cardigan, Kilgetty, adding to my busy programme.

The Shire Hall Hereford has been the regular venue for our rallies for over 25 years, supported by George and Pam Johnson – Jim and Ethel Powell, the brethren being trustees of my ministry.

The Weaver family have also rendered full support. Kath Weaver (Senior) continues to testify of her healing miracle during our very first crusade in Hereford:-

The Story of My Miraculous Healing – by Mrs Weaver

"I live in a small village near Hereford. My early religious connections were with the Parish Church, where I was a member of the Sunday School. Somehow I never experienced a deep relationship with the Lord and I grew up without a knowledge of His wonderful salvation. Some years ago I began to be troubled with acute pain in my back. Finally I decided to consult my local doctor who advised me to see a specialist. The X-Ray revealed that I had contracted tuberculosis of the spine and I was confined to a hospital bed for eight months.

My body was placed in a plaster cast and my limbs were bandaged to the bed. Only my head was permitted to move freely. This was followed by three months in an ordinary bed which meant a total of twelve months lying on my back. The specialist informed me later that three vertebrae were affected. I was resultantly fitted with a spinal support which I wore for five years until God miraculously healed me. In addition I was obliged to walk around with the aid of two sticks. At times the pain was intense and unbearable.

I shall never forget the wonderful miracle which took place in my body during early 1962. I had never witnessed a Divine Healing service, in fact I was quite sceptical about it all. That is until the power of God fell upon me and I was cured. The Crusade Services were being held in the Hereford Town Hall. My sister invited me along to hear Evangelist

Peter Scothern. A wonderful presence met me as I entered the hall I knew God was behind Brother Scothern's anointed ministry.

Positive Prayer Offered

I remember very little of the first part of the service, but the message inspired me and that evening Brother Scothern prayed a mass prayer instructing the sick to lay hands upon themselves.

I stood and placed my right hand upon my spine where the pain troubled me most. As he prayed the power of God came upon me. It seemed like a heated sensation and there were tiny movements in my back as if a supernatural hand was passing over it. I knew I was healed and on arriving home I removed my spinal support and discovered the cure was complete.

The following week I was X-Rayed and notified that my spine was healed. Again this year I have been thoroughly examined and declared completely cured.

In sheer gratitude to the Lord who has saved and healed me I was baptised in water. Jesus has been wonderful to me and I will praise Him forever.

"Whatever your need, however serious your case. He is able to do exceeding abundantly above all that you are able to ask or even think."

Our regular visits to Bath have been one of the highlights of my crusade ministry. David and Elizabeth Way have always given dedicated support proving to be faithful friends over many years. David is pastor of the Corn Street Mission in the centre of the city, where he is highly respected.

The Elizabeth Way Miracle

Elizabeth experienced her miracle from Jesus some years ago. She was suddenly stricken with Rheumatoid Arthritis, which rapidly spread throughout her body. In despair she was extremely troubled, imagining she might be confined to a wheelchair. All the joy went out of her life.

David persuaded her to attend one of my monthly meetings encouraging her to trust in the Lord's deliverance.

Elizabeth was blessed a number of times. On each occasion she received encouragement from the Lord. Slowly but surely the condition began to subside. Her faith greatly increased and after a few months the arthritic affliction completely disappeared. Jesus triumphed and Elizabeth is a living witness to Christ's power to heal today.

Often when I visit Birmingham the Lord reveals His miraculous grace and power to the hundreds who attend the Saturday night deliverance rallies at the Hockley Pentecostal Church, Lodge Road. Miles and Judy Witherford now pastor the assembly following years of loyal service rendered by the late Miss Reeves and Miss Fisher.

I remember God healing an elderly Christian stricken with a stroke. Within moments of the prayer of faith he was marching up and down the aisle like a soldier on parade with tears of joy streaming down his face. A young fellow lame in one leg suddenly jumped to his feet and raced round the assembly like a greyhound. Everyone came alive with clapping hands and shouts of praise. But the highlight of my 35 years ministry at Hockley has been the spontaneous response to the gospel appeal. My heart melts to see folk of all ages, nationalities and background kneeling at the front to receive Jesus as their Saviour. Praise God for Miles and Judy remaining faithful to the heavenly vision. Of course I have another favourite venue in Birmingham – the Homeland Mission Hall Balsall Heath, now faithfully pastored by Olive Everitt. I remember Olive's dedicated parents in the later 40's when they established the Book and Tract Depot.

Blessed Cloth Miracles

It is the anointing that breaks the yoke and this is certainly evident through the prayer cloth ministry.

> *"And God wrought special miracles by the hands of Paul: So that from his body were brought unto the sick handkerchiefs or aprons, and the diseases departed from them, and the evil spirits went out of them."*

(Acts 19:11-12)

Over the years I have received numerous requests for prayer cloths from many nations overseas.

From Poland came an urgent request for a blessed prayer cloth from the family of a mother stricken with T.B. She had been seriously ill for some months and they despaired of her life.

Upon receiving the anointed prayer cloth it was laid upon the mother in the name of the Lord Jesus. From that hour the dying woman made an amazing recovery and the news of her miraculous healing reached the village where she lived. Giving testimony to the glory of God she was inundated with requests to use the same prayer cloth to bless others in need. One by one the Lord healed many sick and suffering until there was a great crowd of witnesses declaring the wonderful works of the Lord. God established a testimony in that place through the simple means of the prayer cloth ministry.

Frequently while conducting divine healing services I am asked to pray over a handkerchief in the name of the Lord Jesus. Generally these are used for the healing of the sick and suffering. A caring mother brought a handkerchief to be blessed for her young son afflicted with asthma. The Lord healed the boy and we added another testimony to our files. Requests for the prayer cloths frequently arrive from Africa and India. These are used by national evangelists or pastors engaged in the deliverance ministry. I receive many encouraging testimonies sometimes supported by photographs of those healed and delivered.

I give God all the praise and glory for every miracle of grace and healing wrought in the Name of the Wonderful Son of God.

3

Miracles of Grace

There is no greater miracle than life itself. All the more wonderful that God placed natural life in a tiny seed. Certainly the miracle of germination remains one of the marvels of creation.

It is difficult to believe that a mighty oak can grow from a tiny acorn, or that a full grown human developes from a tiny seed.

But that is the mystery of the miracle of creation. Similarly the Holy Spirit "seeds" the Kingdom of God in our hearts. The new birth becomes a reality the moment the Holy Spirit "seeds" the nature of Jesus in our lives. We are "born again" of incorruptable seed which is the WORD OF GOD (LOGOS) – the living CHRIST who lives and abides forever. The ongoing ministry of the Holy Spirit is to continually seed the Kingdom of God. Jesus said, *"The Kingdom of God is WITHIN US."* (Luke 17:21). Likewise the ministry of every "born again" believer is to "seed" the Kingdom of God in the lives of others. This is accomplished through testimony, preaching, praying and daily living. I have known the Kingdom of God be "seeded" through a smile, a handshake, a prayer, a telephone call, a kind deed, a word in season, a letter of consolation, and in numerous other ways.

At such times we must exercise total confidence in the Holy Spirit to faithfully "watch over" the seed that has been sown. It has been my humble joy to seed the Kingdom of God these past forty years in the lives of others.

I distinctly recall my first visit to the market town of Hadleigh in Suffolk. One evening a young man challenged by the gospel ministry surrendered his life to Christ. This youthful firebrand was soon in zealous action evangelizing his community. I have known Don Double over thirty years and praise God for his advancement in the ministry. The Kingdom of God was soundly seeded in his young heart by the Holy Ghost.

I remember my first encounter with Anne and Trevor Dearing. It was my humble privilege to witness the Holy Ghost seed their ministries.

I spent many long hours travelling to St. Paul's Hainault during the years 1971-76. It was my great joy to participate in the initial stages of the Hainault visitation. The "seeds" of God's grace are miracles indeed.

Saul of Tarsus encountered the risen Christ on the Damascus highway. This was to change his life, his person and his destiny. God seeded His Kingdom in Saul's heart. Saul the destroyer became Paul the Apostle – a miracle of divine grace. Peter, James and John were also recipients of the same amazing grace "seeded" in their hearts by the Lord Jesus. Likewise Matthew the tax gatherer, along with Mary Magdelene the prostitute, and Nicodemus the religionist.

My life was similarly transformed by the same miraculous grace. This is the heart miracle of the Christian faith – the conversion of the soul and inner regeneration by the spirit of God. It is all of grace, we are all saved by grace and then kept continually by the same grace. Ours is to trust and obey, but God Himself provides the grace.

I was crusading for Christ on the Isle of Wight. A request was awaiting me to visit Parkhurst maximum security prison. George was serving a life sentence for the murder of his wife. Many years previously George had attended one of my miracle crusades but had turned his back upon God. Some eight weeks later in a rage he battered his wife to death.

Now George was experiencing shocking nightmares, bouts of mental depression and guilt. He welcomed me into his cell and then wept bitterly.

"Can God ever forgive me?" whispered George. "Can God forgive a murderer?"

I told George about the true meaning of the cross and the crucified Saviour. How Jesus had willingly accepted our sins in His body on the tree. The light dawned and George prayed the sinners prayer– repenting, accepting God's forgiveness and surrendering his life to Christ. This life sentence murderer was "born anew." He was gloriously saved by the grace of God.

I learned later that George was assisting the Prison Chaplain and following hard after Jesus.

Elizabeth Meets Jesus

Two deeply distressed parents requested my urgent assistance at the conclusion of one of my church services in Blackpool.

Their teenage daughter Elizabeth was desperately ill with a brain tumour. They escorted me to a fashionable part of town where I found the young lady emaciated and thoroughly weakened by her terrible ordeal. Her hair had disappeared, her cheeks were sunken, and her eyes filled with despair.

I drew a chair along side and asked, "Elizabeth, why do you want me to visit you?"

Bravely holding back her tears she whispered, "I know I am dying. No one has told me but I know it's true. I've been brought up to go to church and last year I became a Sunday School teacher, I've tried to be a good Christian and always do the right things, I always thought when you believed in God and you were dying that God's presence and peace would be very real. Well it's not, and I feel so afraid of dying and God seem's a million miles away.

Please help me to find peace and assurance!"

There are many folk like Elizabeth, hoping to find divine peace and assurance through good works and spiritual efforts. Even devout church goers can miss the assurance of salvation. I speak from experience.

At the age of seventeen years, after regularly attending church, I suddenly realised I was dying without peace and assurance. It took the reality of death to bring me to this all important conclusion.

Elizabeth readily accepted the basic principles of the gospel.

First – she recognised that she was a SINNER, needing God's forgiveness.

Secondly – she realized her good works and religious up bringing were not sufficient to save her.

Thirdly – she believed Jesus died on the cross bearing her sins in His own body according to the scriptures. (1 Peter 2:24).

At this point Elizabeth took a step she had never taken before. She reverently bowed her head in prayer, asking Christ to forgive all her sins. She thanked Him in return. Then she invited the living Jesus into her heart to reign within as Lord and Saviour. It was the personal acceptance of Christ which bought the peace and assurance.

Immediately she *knew* she was saved. She *knew* she was forgiven.

Her face radiated with peace and the joy of Salvation.

Christ had come into her heart.

Four days later Elizabeth died. Just before her triumphant passing she said with a radiant smile, "I see Jesus coming to fetch me, mother, father. I'm going to heaven! I will see you again soon."

A few weeks later Elizabeth's parents attended one of my gospel services to make the same commitment to Christ. Every person saved, forgiven and born again of God's Spirit is a MIRACLE OF HIS SAVING GRACE.

The ongoing ministry of the Holy Spirit is to convict us of sin until we sincerely repent. Then he plants in our hearts the seed of the Christ nature. The MIRACLE OF GRACE takes place within our beings. Every true "born again" believer is a MIRACLE OF GRACE. A genuine Christian is a "Jesus person" with the divine nature dwelling within. Oh the wonder of it all – "CHRIST IN US, THE HOPE OF GLORY!"

"And because we are Sons, God hath sent forth the Spirit of His Son INTO YOUR HEARTS, CRYING, ABBA FATHER" (Gal. 4:6).

I repeat it again and again with joy and assurance – "THE SPIRIT OF THE SON OF GOD IS IN MY HEART."

Oh to recognise this glorious truth AT ALL TIMES, never to forget for one moment that we can experience THE SPIRIT OF GOD'S SON IN OUR HEARTS.

This is the miracle of miracles!

God has made it possible to plant the powerful, pure and holy nature of Jesus within the human heart.

Reader, pause a moment and ask yourself this all important question – "Have I been born again?" If not turn to John Chapter 3 and let God's word illuminate your heart and mind.

GOD WANTS TO IMPART THE DIVINE NATURE OF HIS SON INTO YOUR HEART – TO CHANGE YOU FROM THE INSIDE AND MAKE ALL THINGS NEW.

"Therefore if any man be in CHRIST, he is a new creature: old things are passed away; behold, all things are become new."
(2 Cor. 5:17).

4

Miracles of Divine Healing

Throughout the Bible many miracles of divine healing are recorded. They are a clear indication of God's compassionate concern for sick humanity. Jesus performed remarkable miracles of healing upon the deaf, the blind, and the dumb. He cleansed the lepers, made the lame to walk and cured all manner of sickness and disease. Even after his crucifixion and resurrection Christ continued His ministry of healing through His dedicated disciples. The early apostles performed many signs and wonders in His Name. In Acts chapter 3 Peter and John raised up a crippled man at the gate of the temple Beautiful. Peter also raised Dorcas back to life. At one time Peter's shadow falling upon the sick cured many that were diseased and afflicted.

One direct result of the healing miracles was the conversion of men to Christ. Following the Acts 3 miracles no less than 5,000 believed on the Lord Jesus. That exceeded the number that were saved on the day of Pentecost. I have personally experienced hundreds turning to Christ after God has manifested His miraculous power in the healing of sick and suffering.

The Lord opened the ears of a deaf child during my crusade in Abeokuta, Nigeria, and subsequently hundreds received Christ as Saviour. In Allabad, the seat of Hinduism, God miraculously healed a crippled man. Thousands flocked to hear the gospel once the news of the miracle was known. The Lord opened the eyes of a partially blind housewife in Lampeter, West Wales and hundreds gathered to hear the Word of the Lord. The LIVERPOOL WEEKLY NEWS printed front page headlines – MIRACLES IN DINGLE, and hundreds filled the Wellington Road Baptist Church to hear the gospel and see Christ's power in action.

However, the supreme reason for these divine miracles is the glory of God and the exaltation of the Name of the Lord Jesus. When the crippled man was instantly healed at the gate of the temple Beautiful he ran into the temple, walking, leaping and glorifying God. When Jesus performed miracles men "glorified the God of Israel." Many who are divinely healed in our overseas crusades glorify God from a public platform – while the vast congregations respond with crescendos of praise and thanks to God. Following an outstanding testimony of healing during one of my West Wales crusades the congregation spontaneously arose, clapping their hands, glorifying the Name of the Lord. When a blind native suddenly received his sight in one of my West African crusades thousands began singing praises to Jesus.

Many Outstanding Testimonies

I retain a file filled with written testimonies from those saved, delivered and divinely cured through faith in the Lord Jesus Christ.

There is a glowing account of Glyn's deliverance, a young fellow who was born deaf and dumb, and the remarkable story of Joy Hill's miraculous release from curvature of the spine. There is the enthralling testimony of Mrs. Pitt, totally deaf for thirteen years and the heart-stirring account of the miraculous deliverance of the late Mrs. Annie Towler.

The Annie Towler Story

The late Mrs. Annie Towler of Ingleton was wonderfully transformed and healed by the power of God. This was her personal story.

"From Sunday School days I was a Methodist. I distinctly recall my teacher telling of a miracle of healing in her life which left a deep impression upon my young mind. At the age of eighteen years, I made a decision to serve the Lord, but failed miserably. It took a disturbing domestic situation to bring me to my spiritual senses. I was still attending church but I knew there was something seriously wrong with my life.

I was invited to attend Brother Scothern's special service at Bolton-Le-Sands, where God challenged my heart. I was too self conscious to answer the Gospel appeal, but on arriving home, I sank down on my knees and surrendered myself completely to Jesus. A wonderful peace flooded my soul the following day and it seemed like sunshine filled my heart. I was completely changed by the power of Christ. My terrible temper disappeared and my life became sweet and clear.

Shortly afterwards a second miracle occurred. For twenty years I had suffered acutely with a distressing spinal complaint, through a degenerate disc. I wore a special steel corset to help me get around. I couldn't live without it. Following prayer, I was miraculously healed and discarded my surgical support. For over three years I have enjoyed pain-free health. I am so grateful to the Lord, for all He has done for me."

Mrs. Annie Towler.

My frequent visits to Bath during the last thirty years have resulted in some remarkable incidents. Only recently whilst ministering in Llandrindod Wells I listened to the following testimony.

A young man, Jewish by religion, attended one of our first meetings in Bath. He was a chronic diabetic and attended under pressure from his friends. Upon learning that it was a Christian based meeting he immediately attempted to leave the service but was pressed upon to stay. The initial proceedings held no interest for him, but he was suddenly alerted when through the gift of knowledge I discerned there were diabetics present. To his amazement I personally called upon him stating, "you are also a diabetic needing healing from God." He testified that this approach was so convincing that it was as if Christ Himself had stood before him. The young man was promptly overcome by the Lord's anointing and subsequently experienced a "Saul of Tarsus" conversion and was instantly healed of diabetes. He has served Christ as a missionary to the

Jewish people in South Africa these past twenty years.

David and Elizabeth Way have also supported my ministry in Bath for over twenty years. Elizabeth was suddenly stricken with rheumatoid arthritis some time ago. Her finger was the first part of her anatomy to suffer but the disease quickly spread throughout her body. She dreaded the future and became severely depressed. Elizabeth attended our Bath crusade services and presented herself to the Lord for divine healing through the laying on of hands. I always pray authoritatively in the Name of Jesus for arthritic sufferers. Commanding the infirmity to depart, Elizabeth began to make a slow but certain recovery. Full of appreciation she submitted to water baptism and has radiantly testified to the glory of God since her deliverance.

The picturesque city of Hereford holds many pleasant memories. I served my RAF apprenticeship at Creden Hill during the late 1940's. Jim Powell remembered my first visit to Hereford. I gave my testimony, when in uniform, at the local Apostolic Church. I was to return in the 1960's to conduct a gospel and divine healing crusade in the Town Hall. This proved successful in many ways resulting in a series of monthly meetings in the Shire Hall which continue to the present day.

Loyal and faithful friends including George and Pam Johnson, John and Kath Weaver and family, Jim and Ethel Powell, the late Mr & Mrs Jay, Walter and Margaret Whittall have given their unwavering support.

The late Bill Hale of Newent treasured his contact with the Hereford monthly crusade services. Methodists from Gloucester and Chepstow also experienced renewal during these very lively, Spirit filled meetings. Stephen Parsons, the Anglican clergyman from the nearby village of Lugwardine, was greatly inspired by the healing of his wife Christine during the Hereford monthlies. I was once asked to lecture at the Bishop's Palace on the subject of Divine Healing. Over the years there has been steady in gathering of souls to Christ's Kingdom.

Cyril and Gladys Dimmer once resided locally and gave full support to our Hereford meetings. They now live in West Wales. Gladys faithfully oversees our tract depot, mailing out gospel literature to the four corners of the nation. During one of the memorable revival conventions at Kilgetty in the early 1970's Gladys was miraculously healed. She had worn a surgical jacket for many years following a severe accident during which she fell headlong down a flight of stairs. The specialist informed her that she would never walk again. She was bedridden for many weeks. However, God raised her up, but she was obliged to continue wearing the back support. During the Kilgetty visitation the power of the Holy Spirit fell upon Gladys and when she later removed her surgical jacket she discovered to her amazement that she was every way whole. Her husband Cyril has also been a faithful friend to my ministry over many years. I remember being called to his bedside when he was stricken down with a severe illness. Cyril's faith remained unshaken in the face of intense pain and after laying on of hands in Jesus' Name he promptly rose up in faith and the Lord had worked another miracle. These loyal friends of the ministry once arranged our frequent visits to Weston-Super-Mare having fellowship with the Elim, Assemblies of God and a local Anglican Church.

The first Eastbourne Crusade was conducted in the Town Hall in 1959. The local Committee consisted of dedicated Christians from various churches and assemblies. Syd Thayre, Primrose Franklyn, Harry Gain, Winnie Bridges, Bill and Lucy Talbot, Esme Sinden, Ivy Hill were among that loyal company. This annual event has always been well attended. God's Kingdom has been extended in the salvation of many souls. Sometimes fifty or more have surrendered to Christ either in first time commitment or in rededication. Divine healing has always proved an outstanding feature of the Eastbourne crusades. Scores of sick and suffering have received "the laying on of hands" in the mighty Name of Jesus.

More recently we have welcomed Vaughan Schulze and Don Smith onto the crusade committee. Their contribution has enriched the administration and has also added to the powerful prayer ministry.

Blessed Handkerchief Ministry

One of the most fascinating aspects of my ministry is based upon Acts 19 verses 11-12,

"And God wrought special miracles by the hands of Paul: so that from his body were brought unto the sick handkerchiefs or aprons, and the diseases departed from them, and the evil spirits went out of them."

The apostle Paul would have been inundated with calls for help when God began to use him so effectively. Because it proved impossible to personally attend all calls the Holy Spirit guided Paul to pray over handkerchiefs and aprons to be used as "points of contact" to heal and deliver. No doubt each call would be prayerfully and carefully considered. I don't think there was any question of indiscriminate distribution of these blessed items. They would be given with divine instructions and conditions.

Way back in 1952 I prayed over my first "prayer cloth" and mailed this overseas. I was greatly encouraged to learn that a number of sick natives in a Nigerian village had been cured by the Lord. These days I use an estimate of 5,000 prayer cloths annually. Only recently I received an urgent request to send a blessed prayer cloth to a child dying of an incurable disease in Moscow. I respond to numerous requests from the third world and the resultant testimonies are always soul stirring.

Some years ago I was asked to send a prayer cloth to a Polish mother desperately sick with tuberculosis. She resided in a village with her daughter. There was little hope for her recovery. She received the prayer cloth with profound gratitude and gathered friends and neighbours to pray with her. From that hour she made a remarkable recovery and all gave praise and glory to God. Once the news had travelled others needing healing began to request use of the same little prayer cloth. So one by one the sick were healed and raised up by the wonderful power of God. As many as twenty ailing folk, including a number of children, were restored by Christ's power through the simple ministry of the same little prayer handkerchief. The attitude of the entire village towards God changed and there is a strong Christian testimony in that place to this day.

My files contain many remarkable "prayer handkerchief" testimonies. Tumours have disappeared, cancers have withered, deaf ears unstopped, the blind made to see and demons cast out through the simple but effective New Testament ministry.

A letter from Ghana included a black and white photograph of a well built fellow who was demon possessed and mentally sick. On the reverse side were these words "Delivered by Jesus Christ from demons and insanity through one of your prayer handkerchiefs."

The prayer handkerchiefs are always accompanied by scriptural instructions and texts. They provide an ongoing point of contact and have been greatly used of the Lord for "absent healing." Mothers find them useful for their children and they are also appreciated by the aged who are unable to attend one of my healing services.

Some Christian folk may not agree with this aspect of my ministry but the resultant testimonies are so convincing that I know beyond a shadow of doubt that God still uses this biblical ministry to extend His healing grace to the sick and the suffering.

Some Wonderful Testimonies

"I am writing to tell you about two healings since you sent me three healing cloths some months ago. A niece of mine accepted a blessed cloth as she had arthritis in her spine, she rang me up to tell me she had no further pain in her spine and carries the prayer cloth with her everywhere. Another healing which has taken place is a young woman who had cervical cancer, to whom I gave a blessed cloth. She also specially rang me to say the illness is not troubling her like it used to as she was always experiencing infection and pain. She is believing for full recovery."

Signed, Mrs G. Oliver.

Pastor Gordon Cochrane of Sligo, Ireland, writes:-

"One of my members had a lump on her hand and attended hospital to have it diagnosed. The Specialist drew a purple mark around it and told her to report again. Meanwhile, I gave her one of your blessed prayer cloths which she applied in the Lord's Name. The offending LUMP SUDDENLY DISAPPEARED and when she reported to the hospital all that remained was the purple ring. The Specialist was greatly surprised."

Our testimony files contain many thrilling stories from those blessed, saved and healed through the "prayer cloth" ministry. TO GOD BE ALL THE GLORY!

5

Miracles in India

I was called by the Lord to India during the 1960's. The business of finding the required finance presented a real challenge to my faith. Nevertheless I could not take this important decision without much prayer and consultation with the Word of the Lord.

I can say in truth, "THY WORD, O LORD, IS A LAMP UNTO MY FEET AND A LIGHT TO MY PATH." The Lord indeed opened the way by invitation to crusade in the great city of Allahabad, the seat of Hinduism. Pastor Sylvester of the local Full Gospel Church made most of the arrangements for this visit. So it was that I took the platform before a locally estimated congregation of around 35,000. Most were Hindus with a few Europeans. This memorable crusade was to last five days. Streaming from all parts of the city and suburbs of Allahabad thousands came to listen to the Word of God. The Lord enabled me to faithfully preach the gospel of repentance and salvation with great power and persuasion. Many were convicted in heart and accepted the basic truths of the gospel.

There was an almost unbelievable response to the salvation call as hundreds raised their hands and earnestly prayed to be saved. Mass prayer for the sick followed. Scores of deaf and dumb were healed and made to hear and speak. New ear drums were created. Totally deaf ears were able to hear the slightest whisper. So effective were the miracles wrought on the deaf that they were seen holding hands to their ears because the shock on new found hearing proved too much for them.

Vast Multitudes Attend

Pressing invitations arrived to crusade in other towns and cities throughout India. A vast multitude, estimated by the authorities at around 75,000, thronged the Circus park outside of Calcutta. New Testament scenes were witnessed nightly as hundreds professed a new found faith in Christ, the Lord confirming His Word with signs following. Many evenings during the proceedings those bound and oppressed with evil spirits would cry out. The demon possessed were frequently escorted to the platform where under an intense anointing of the Holy Spirit I performed numerous deliverances.

It was estimated that 80% of the thousands present were listening to the Gospel for the first time. Vast supplies of Christian literature and tracts were distributed. Weeks after I returned to England the crowds continued to congregate in the circus grounds where Indian evangelists and ministers continued to preach the ways of the Lord.

Nearly twenty years later the results of these amazing mass gospel and healing crusades continue to come to light. Some months ago I was ministering in the Essex area. An Indian gentleman approached me towards the end of the evening service. "You will no doubt have forgotten me," he remarked. "I was crossing the Circus park in Calcutta many years ago and my little daughter was bitten by a scorpion. I gathered the little one in my arms. Her limbs were beginning to swell and she was crying with pain. I saw a group of men and I rushed over. You saw my urgent need, took my little girl in your arms and claimed healing in the name of Jesus Christ. To my astonishment my little girl was miraculously cured and although at that time I was a devout Hindu I became a Christian. I am living and working in England now and I belong to a Pentecostal Church but my experience with Christ began that wonderful morning when Jesus healed my daughter through your faithful prayers."

The Blind See

A young man of 26 years, suffering from blurred vision, threw his heavy lenses into the crowd around him, shouting that he could see perfectly. Many blind were made to see following the healing prayers offered in Jesus' Name. A young boy of seven years was miraculously healed of a twisted arm and raised it up for the crowd to see. A paralytic who lay in front of the platform unable to move, suddenly started walking, screaming for joy!! Shouts of "Jishu Masih Ki Ja!" meaning "Praise to Jesus Christ" rent the evening air as thousands saw the paralytic made whole. He was a Christian gentleman of fifty one years unable to walk owing to a compound fracture of the kneecap. Following the miracle he stepped up to the platform and gave a glowing testimony to the glory of Jesus Christ.

A schoolgirl brought seventy miles and blind in both eyes was perfectly restored. A young boy with stammering tongue was miraculously restored and made to speak clearly and distinctly. The multitude voiced their praise in a crescendo of "hallelujah's."

The Deaf Miraculously Restored

An excited mother held up her child. He had been completely deaf following a fever attack. After prayer in Jesus Name he could hear a whisper. A woman beaming with joy told how a cancer had instantly disappeared from her breast. Her friends confirmed the miracle. A schoolgirl wept as she told how Jesus had restored her eyesight. A young man waving his right arm proved that the Lord had restored his paralysed arm. Arthritics jumped up and down to reveal what Christ had done for them. A crippled native related how he could walk again after twelve years. The crowds responded with shouts of joy. Hindus having received the Lord Jesus told of their happiness in the Lord. At times the platform became so crowded with folk desiring to testify that it became impossible to continue with the service. Most meetings concluded with an over-crowded platform of excited, praising folk all anxious to give testimony to the glory of God.

The Tapus Dutt Miracle

Outside Calcutta stands a spacious auditorium used for great events, celebrations and public gatherings. A vast company numbering tens of thousands filled this venue. Like a vast harvest field the well ordered assembly listened intently to every word. With forthright clarity I proclaimed the story of Jesus, commanding repentance and faith through His name. Thousands shared the "prayer of salvation" turning their lives over to the authority of the Lord Jesus. Spiritual joy and rejoicing followed as the reality of the new life in Christ became apparent.

I then offered positive and authoritative prayer for the sick and suffering. The hushed congregation reverently bowed their heads sharing the healing prayer. In the all powerful Name of Jesus the infirmities and afflictions present were positively rebuked and exorcised.

A Helpless Cripple

Somewhere in the rear, approximately three hundred yards from the platform, lay a young man crippled and disabled. He had never stood upright in his life. His balloon-like legs were terribly distorted and deformed. He was obliged to drag his body along the ground with the aid of wooden blocks. He had existed for eighteen years in this horizontal position. Could there have been in this great multitude anyone needing God's miracle more than this crippled youth? Tapus Dutt sincerely subscribed to every detail of the healing prayer. Previously he had responded to the "salvation prayer" and his heart was already filled with an unspeakable joy and peace. Now he prepared for an even greater miracle.

What follows is best related by those who personally witnessed the amazing TAPUS DUTT MIRACLE. During the devout silence, broken only by the healing prayer, strange sounds began to emerge from the crippled youth as he lay on the ground. These abnormal noises continued for about sixty seconds. They were immediately followed by a loud crackling sound which drew the attention of all in the vicinity. Amazed and astonished onlookers witnessed an unbelievable sight. As Tapus began taking sharp intakes of breath his deformed swollen limbs rapidly lost their volume and began supernaturally taking on their natural shape and character. Everyone who witnessed this amazing event was held spellbound. Then one and another fell upon their knees excitedly giving glory to God with outbursts of praise and thanksgiving.

An Amazing Phenomena

Tapus ran his hands over his newly formed limbs. Tears of joy flowed down his cheeks. Trembling with excitement he struggled to his feet.

Eager hands came to assist him. Supported by his jubilant compatriots he was half carried towards the crusade platform. Demanding to be released, he was set to the ground, and to everyone's amazement began walking upright. Unsteady at first, his confidence regained, Tapus flung himself before the platform emitting incoherent torrents of praise and thanks in his native tongue.

With intense excitement the facts were quickly pieced together. TAPUS DUTT'S HELPLESSLY DEFORMED AND DISTORTED LIMBS HAD BEEN MIRACULOUSLY RE-CREATED BY A MIRACLE OF GOD. The news spread like prairie fire and soon the entire assembly were worshipping and blessing the Name of Jesus. I warmly embraced the youth and recorded the details. Within twenty four hours the astonishing Tapus Dutt miracle occupied the headlines in the Indian media.

I eventually left Calcutta to travel back to England. So great was the impact of this gospel crusade that the services continued at the circus grounds for another ten weeks conducted by local pastors and evangelists.

Some five years following the Calcutta crusade one of the converts, a young Hindu, travelled to North India to preach the gospel. A missionary from England told the following story:

"I was appointed by my missionary council to visit and evangelise the villages of North India. I was informed there were no Christian churches in that area. Upon arrival I discovered a group of Christian assemblies in one particular locality. Upon close questioning I discovered that a young ex-Hindu evangelist had pioneered the gospel to this group of evangelical villages. The young evangelist was converted to Christ during the Peter Scothern crusade in Calcutta." To God be the glory!

6

Miracles in Africa

It was during a visit to the U.S.A. that I experienced an almost unbelievable encounter with a heavenly emissary.

The Crusade was conducted in the Metropolitan Opera House in Philadelphia before a company of 7,000 people. Saturday was a day of rest from the normal routine but I was constrained to spend the afternoon in prayer within the solitude of the empty theatre. Quietly meditating within the shadows of the spacious platform, I was suddenly aware of a presence. Looking up I saw someone standing about twelve feet away. Presuming the person to be one of the lady attendants I enquired, "Can I help you?" For a few moments there was complete silence and then the most beautiful voice gave forth a prophetic utterance that caused me to tingle from head to toe. Then as suddenly as the being had appeared so it faded into the shadows.

This supernatural happening completely mystified me. I rose up and examined the platform area and then the entire building calling, "Are you there?"

The building remained empty and deserted. Returning to the platform the phenomena occurred again. The same being, the same message, and once again the visitor melted into the shadows but the message remained indelibly imprinted upon my mind. It was a call to take the gospel of the Kingdom with power to West Africa.

Call To West Africa

Returning to England I received an airmail letter inviting me to conduct a large scale crusade in Sierra Leone exactly as the heavenly visitor had indicated.

Within weeks I was en route to West Africa and arrived in Freetown during the January, an ideal month for open air meetings. All local churches were invited to co-operate in a town-wide Gospel Crusade which eventually attracted crowds of around 10,000 or more to the Central Queen Victoria Park.

The multitude overflowed into the nearby streets and so the police were drafted in to cope with the problem. People flocked in from the countryside using every conceivable means of transport. Some using trucks and lorries, others by cycle and car and many on foot walking distances of up to fifty miles. Many families actually camped on the Crusade ground and throughout the night little fires were burning in every corner of the campus. Children climbed the nearby trees and pylons, while the coaches were conveniently parked so that their roofs were used for extra seating.

Mass Gospel Service

These mass gospel services were a continual scene of New Testament blessing and revival. Hundreds claimed a new found faith in Christ, most of them hearing the gospel for the very first time. The prayers for salvation were sincerely repeated by large sections of the vast congregation. Those deciding to follow the Lord were shepherded into the local Brethren church for special counselling. Some evenings the Church was filled three times over with enquirers. Counselling continued frequently until well past midnight. Numerous lives were influenced and changed as the Lord's message went forth in the power and demonstration of the Holy Ghost. It was just like a scene from the Book of Acts. The power and presence of Jesus filled the evening air. Miracles occurred in abundance.

One evening the great service was interrupted when a blind beggar suddenly received his sight and began joyfully screaming, "I can see the stars! I can see the stars!." A lame woman, partially paralysed, was dramatically cured while she listened to the early testimonies. She jumped up in the midst of the assembly praising God with a loud voice. Eventually she was assisted to the platform and proceeded to demonstrate her healing while the multitude shared their delight with praise and thanksgiving.

The Sierra Leone "Daily Mail" published repeated reports of the crusade including the healing miracles. No less than four whole pages of testimonies appeared in one edition. Headlines on posters, press and radio re-affirmed the mighty work of grace wrought through faith in Christ. Some evenings as many as fifty or more would clamber to the platform to testify of divine healing from every kind of affliction. The deaf were made to hear, the blind to see and the dumb to speak. The lame would leap for joy. One blind Freetown man of 82 years received new sight and his amazing story appeared in the centre pages of the "Daily Mail."

A God Inspired Earth Tremor

One evening the power of God was so in evidence, that during my prayer for the sick the crusade ground literally shook and hundreds were thrown to the floor. The newspapers the following day reported the earth tremor.

Perhaps one of the most dramatic scenes occurred during the exorcism of evil spirits. The demons would cry out as I stood to minister the Word of God. I would first bind and then release the demon possessed with power and authority just like Jesus and His disciples. The scenes that followed were indescribable as the Holy Spirit dealt effectively with the offending evil forces.

"Preach the gospel! Heal the sick! Cast out devils! Cleanse the lepers! Raise the dead!" were my Master's orders and through His grace and power I implicitly obeyed.

Cleanse Lepers

I was en route to the racecourse in Ibadan when I passed a group of lepers painfully journeying to the evening crusade. One woman was in a serious condition. The gaping wound on her leg was covered with flies. I'm certain I could see the white of the bone. I noticed she was wearing a dirty head turban and her back was bent as she leaned precariously upon a stout bamboo. As I passed this motley company of suffering humanity the words of the Lord Jesus signalled my mind "CLEANSE THE LEPERS." I was always mystified by the command. I did not understand what Jesus meant **"CLEANSE** the lepers."

You can imagine my intense joy and surprise at the conclusion of the meeting when this same woman was escorted to the platform following the divine healing session. On the fringe of the multitude the Lord's power reached her with amazing consequences. Her diseased leg was perfectly restored. I could hardly believe my eyes. New flesh filled the gaping wound. It was pinkish in colour and contrasted with the rest of her limbs. She was beside herself with gratitude and a local pastor explained to her that it was God's power and not mine that had performed this amazing cure. Once the truth had dawned upon those present a crescendo of praise ascended which shook the crusade ground and echoed around the surrounding locality. I came to the conclusion that the cleansing of this poor leper was none other than a miraculous demonstration of God's great grace and mercy. Jesus' compassion had overflowed to the far corners of the needy assembly and the leper woman had caught the impact in her diseased body.

There were other occasions when lepers were seen in my vast crusade. Some would attend alone but generally they came in small groups. I was particularly moved in heart when I saw children afflicted with the disease, but most were adults in the later stages. Unlike Bible days when they were isolated from society these were seen flowing in company with the tide of humanity making it's way to the crusade venues. Most were severely crippled and presented a pathetic sight. I was always moved with compassion as they appeared forlorn and forsaken. I could picture Jesus full of concern and compassion for the lepers in New Testament days. I heard of others who were healed and made well by the Lord's power during my third world crusades but found them to be a shy and a reserved people and therefore a problem to get them to testify in public. This one thing I do know, that lepers were healed and cleansed by the mighty power of God and that the Lord's name was glorified among these people.

The Abeokuta Crusade

We arrived at the Palace Grounds, Abeokuta, half an hour before the commencement of the service. An expectant crowd of 800 or more thronged around the platform. Police faced great difficulties with the excited multitude as they pressed towards the platform. The numbers rapidly increased until about 1,000 or more were present. His Highness – the Alake of Abeokuta – occupied his chair on the palace balcony. The great meeting commenced. I gave everyone a warm welcome from all the churches, religions and denominations. I further acknowledged (with gratitude) the presence of His Highness. Declaring that Jesus Christ was the Son of God, and able to perform miracles to prove His resurrection from the dead, I requested a little girl at random from the sick compound. She was totally deaf in both ears and her sister guided her to the platform. With authority I prayed..."That everyone present may know and believe that Jesus Christ is the son of the True and Living God I command these ears to open in the name of Jesus." Instantly God performed the miracle. To everyone's astonishment she could hear perfectly. This was proved as she began to repeat the sounds and words. There was a breathless silence from the multitude. Then followed a roar of united praise. For five minutes confusion prevailed. The excited multitude raised clouds of dust as they danced for joy. The young girl was promptly conveyed to His Highness who showed full approval to the miracle.

After a difficult period of confusion order was restored and the great crowd listened intently to fine faithbuilding Bible message calling them to salvation in Jesus Christ. "God has no favourites," I declared. "He can do the same for you if you believe."

The message was climaxed with conviction and a great Gospel appeal during which 450 raised their hands to denote their decision for Christ. Then followed a PANARAMO OF MIRACLES when 35 deaf mutes joyfully testified of healing and restoration of hearing. The multitude grew so excited they stormed the platform and it became impossible to continue. We pressed towards home through the jubilant crowds singing and shouting praises to God.

2,500 Professed a New Living Faith in Christ in Four Days!

Excited multitudes rushed the platform after witnessing unforgettable miracles!

News of Christ's miracles spread like a fire. Parties journied 200 miles to swell the mass meetings to 6,000 or more. Over 2,500 professed a new living faith in Christ in the first great four meetings. These were unforgettable scenes. Many waited all night under the stars for the next service. Faith ran higher than ever. They stood for hours under the fierce equatorial sun drinking in the words of life and faith.

Distorted, pain racked bodies filled the compound. We assured them soundly from the scriptures of God's willingness to save and heal everyone. In a soul stirring appeal no less than 1,000 souls made a first time decision for Christ. I repeated the salvation instructions, should they have misunderstood the message and call to repentance. They had not. The response was just the same.

A Famous African King Testifies...

Since the Ilesha Miracle Crusade commenced I have been able to attend many of the services. Both my wife and myself have been profoundly stirred by the things we have seen and heard. Little deaf children have been instantly made to hear. Blind people have been able to see again. Many sick and diseased have been healed by the prayer of faith. I have witnessed these miracles night by night.

Hundreds have gathered in the Palace Courtyard and many have professed a new found faith in Christ. None could doubt the power of God in these services. The Bible messages have been inspiring and faith building. The multitude have rejoiced exceedingly in God's faithfulness to fulfil His promises.

On the second night of the Crusade both my wife and I renewed our consecretation to Christ in a personal way. The Lord has also touched my body through the prayers of Rev. Scothern and Rev. Williams.

I pray that God will continue to bless the team wherever they go and that thousands more will be blessed and healed through their ministry.

Adelupougunnokun Biladu 111, Owa of Ilesha.

7

Miracles Among the Demon Possessed

Loosing The Legions

Two thousand years ago, Jesus stood on the banks of
the Sea of Galilee, across from the ancient land of
Gadara. Shortly afterwards ensued one of the most
horrific spiritual conflicts on record in the Bible.
Suddenly there appeared a wild, naked man,
emerging from the "Valley of Tombs." Screaming at
the top of his voice with the fires of insanity flaming
in his eyes, he threw himself in an uncontrollable
frenzy upon the little company of disciples.

Jesus Masters a Madman

Legion was his name. He was a notorious demon
possessed madman, who roamed the countryside,
bringing fear and terror to the populace. He was
possessed with so many demons that no man could
tame him. When they tried to bind him, he would
snap the chains asunder. The wild man drew himself
to his full height, screamed hideously and plunged
forward to attack. Then suddenly he saw Jesus. The
demon powers cringed within him. They trembled
with fear. They screamed out in holy terror – "Jesus,

thou Son of God, I know thee, who thou art. Hast thou come to torment us before our time?" In His authoritative, compelling voice, Jesus said, "What is thy Name?" The maniac answered, "My name is LEGION, for we are many." Jesus said, "I command thee, thou unclean spirit, come out of him, come out of him!" Legion shouted cursed and shrieked. He leaped into the air and crashed to the ground. He writhed, wriggled and twisted like a serpent. Then his huge hands relaxed, the fires of insanity faded from his eyes, and he lay motionless on the ground.

Legion of Gadara Loosed

Jesus took him by the hand, and lifted him up. Looking around in obvious amazement, he gazed up at Jesus. "Master! Master!" he cried. "I am free! I am loosed! You have made me whole!" Jesus said, "Get him some clothes." Legion was soon on his way rejoicing, clothed and in his right mind. He was delivered by the mighty ministry of Jesus of Nazareth.

Legions Exist Today

People have the strange idea that demon powers passed away with Bible days. During my international missionary journeys, time and time again, I have been confronted with demon possessed individuals. I have witnessed similar manifestations of evil as recorded in the story of Legion. I have known these uncanny powers toss a human body around like a cork. They have held conversations with me, they have cursed me, and tried on many occasions to attack me.

I was ministering in Yorkshire and was requested to interview a demented woman who had been a mental case for two years. She kept hearing voices, strange unclean voices. Eventually the demon possessed her and spoke through her. During my interview she appeared perfectly normal. Suddenly her eyes went wild. She began clawing and scratching herself, tearing at her clothing. A man's voice began cursing me. The voice came from her throat and not through her mouth. She never opened her lips once. The unclean spirit actually possessed her vocal chords, and spoke through her. I commanded the demon to hold its peace, and she collapsed to the ground. Screaming hideously, the spirit came out from her. I am not suggesting that all mentally sick people are demon possessed, but I want to prove beyond doubt that there are still many bound by such influences who can be set free by the mighty power of God.

During an eventful crusade on the south coast I encountered my first challenging case of demon possession.

One of the officiating ministers of a local church urgently requested my interest in an Indian family. Their teenage daughter was under the control of some sinister influence which would ruthlessly cast her to the floor. I visited the home and the first fifteen minutes passed uneventfully. The father provided the background history of the case while the girl sat unconcerned reading a secular magazine. Throughout the exercise I kept a watchful eye on her.

This proved a wise precaution, for suddenly, without warning, the girl hurled the magazine in my direction. It was only the timely intervention of the father that prevented the estranged daughter from falling upon me. Her eyes were aflame with evil with her face twisted and contorted. She wrestled violently with her father and eventually broke free.

I was anticipating the full impact as she lurched towards me. Suddenly the girl fell to the floor as the invisible power of God prevented her from making contact with me.

Divine Protection

I have experienced this remarkable protection on many occasions. It seemed as if she had run into a plate glass window. For a while she lay completely stunned and silent. Then she began groaning. A gurgling sound emerged followed by a deep gruff voice. "She is mine, I have her, she is mine." We were listening to the voice of a demon! There was no evidence of her lips moving. The sound seemed to come from the pit of her stomach.

For a few moments I was rather hesitant, having never faced a situation quite like this. Gradually I became aware of a spiritual resentment of the evil power which had spoilt this young life. "In the Name of Jesus, my Lord and Master, I bind you, I bind you!" I defiantly prayed. Then it seemed as if a supernatural hand lifted me up and placed me alongside her.

To my further amazement the sinister voice retorted, "She is mine, I will not leave her, she is mine." "Oh yes you will!" I replied with an authoritative voice, "In the Name of God's Son, Jesus Christ, come out of the woman." There was a subtle change in her attitude. "Do let me stay here, please let me stay, she is mine." I sensed that victory was near. "In the Name of Jesus, I command you to come out of her." She began writhing like a serpent on the floor when suddenly her body seemed to lift about a foot from the ground and then she collapsed in a heap. She gave a hideous scream and lay limp, like a dead person. Her father fell to his knees to comfort her. The battle was over. Jesus had triumphed, glory to His Mighty Name! Within seconds she opened her eyes and gazed around. Her eyes were clear and normal. They lifted her on to a settee, where, for a few moments she appeared dazed and bewildered. "Where am I? What has happened?" she enquired in broken English. "Into God's care," replied her father.

She was radiantly happy now and thrilled to be released. We gave thanks together, rendering unto Jesus the praise and the glory for her dramatic deliverance. I left the home greatly appreciative of Christ's power and certainly made wiser by this traumatic experience.

The Study of Demons

This event impressed upon me the desire to begin a diligent study of demonology, and the scriptures offered a real source of inspiration and enlightenment.

I came to understand that demons were evil earth bound personalities craving animal or human embodiment. Their expressed intention is to afflict, vex, oppress and eventually destroy their victims. They are wandering, homeless, disfranchised beings, seeking rest and finding none. They are a plague to human society and Jesus during His powerful ministry proved their existence beyond doubt. The demons of today are not a new race but simply the same twisted evil beings which Jesus and His disciples had to contend with in New Testament days. They fearfully revere and obey the superior authority invested in the all powerful Name of Jesus.

Another Amazing Exorcism

During another exorcism I was to learn even more of the sinister workings of these defamed beings from the spirit world. A young woman, tormented and harassed, attended one of the Central London crusades. The deliverance was conducted under strict medical supervision in the presence of a nurse. During the initial proceedings the violent spirit threw the young woman to the floor, whereupon she began to cry out, "She is mine! She is mine! I will not come out of her!"

The voice of the demon was loud and clear. I responded by making mention of the precious blood of Jesus Christ. Whereupon, the foul spirit tore the young woman ruthlessly shrieking, "I hate the blood of Jesus! I hate the blood of Jesus!" Eventually the demon spirit departed with a shout leaving its victim prostrate on the ground.

When the young woman recuperated she had no knowledge of what had transpired. The nurse assisted her to a chair where she sat quietly for a while. The grateful woman was released from every vestige of the evil influence and returned home normal and well. I recently learned that she is now happily married with a little family and faithfully attending a church on the south coast.

During another Central London meeting the evening service was suddenly interrupted by a young man crying out, "Torment me not, Jesus, torment me not." One of the stewards promptly went to assist the troubled youth. I invited the congregation to join in the prayerful singing of "There is power in the blood, power in the blood, in the precious blood of the Lamb." It was obvious by now that the young fellow was enslaved by a strong and powerful influence. Again came the agonising cry, "Torment me not, Jesus, torment me not!"

Under a mighty anointing of the Holy Spirit I charged the evil power to be silent. I also detected a black outline surrounding the young man. Taking absolute authority over the offending influence I commanded the spirit to depart. Slowly but certainly the strange darkened mist hovering around the youth drifted away moving towards a nearby window and evaporated into the night. The youth lay motionless for a while. Following a further word of command from me the youth rose to his feet completely whole. The congregation burst into spontaneous praise glorifying the Lord for such a powerful demonstration of His grace and mercy.

Home Exorcism

I was also called upon to exorcise an unclean spirit from a house haunted by a poltergeist. There was no doubt about this because of the mischievous character of the unclean fiend. The desperate housewife discovered a number of dirty marks on her clean walls which she proceeded to erase with much care. However, the marks re-appeared again and again even when the walls were newly decorated. There seemed to be no logical explanation to these uncanny happenings. By this time the young housewife was beside herself with worry and fear. I explained exactly what had caused the problem and proceeded to bind and exorcise the troublesome spirit. The windows were opened wide and positive prayer offered. From that hour there was no further evidence of the unclean influence.

A further case involved the invasion by tormenting spirits of a nursing home. The nursing staff as well as the patients were the victims of many weird and fearful happenings. I was invited to stay overnight in order to assess the problem and carry out a successful exorcism in the Name of the Lord Jesus. Around midnight the household was awakened by a series of cries from one of the nurses' rooms. Upon opening the door she was found lying on the floor having been dragged out of bed by some powerful and invisible force. She was trembling with fear and the staff comforted her with prayer and a hot drink. No one returned to bed that evening and time was spent in prayer and consideration of the problem.

I was distinctly guided to a certain room in the house which seemed to be the source of the problem. The staff nurse later testified that this was the only room in the house that the kitten would not enter. After a service of exorcism and rededication the house was cleansed of the evil. It was later ascertained that the church nearby had also been subject to black magic ritual.

I have often been awakened in the early hours by pastors and ministers seeking my counsel and assistance with exorcism problems.

How I Detect A Demon

During my international ministry, time and time again I have been confronted by the demon obsessed and possessed. The most remarkable incidents have occurred when I have positively preached the resurrection of Jesus Christ from the dead. The Bible says,

> *"And with great power gave the aspostles witness of the resurrection of the Lord Jesus: and great grace was upon them all."*

(Acts 4:33)

Amazing Exorcism

One evening, during the recent Indian Crusades, after quoting the above verse from the Book of Acts, a high school mistress was thrown down to the ground. The convulsive demons shook her body like serpent and hissed through her mouth. Wriggling furiously she was carried to the platform.

> *"For unclean spirits, crying the loud voice, came out of many that were possessed with them: and many taken with palsies, and that were lame were healed."*

(Acts 8:7)

I tested the spirits and tried them according to 1 John 4:1-3. They refused to make a positive confession of the physical resurrection of Jesus Christ from the grave. I promptly discerned that the unfortunate woman was deceived by her contacts with spiritism. The demons, realising they were exposed, screamed out but were obliged to leave after my authoritative command in Jesus' Name.

After her recovery, the School Mistress accepted Christ, and confessed her belief in the literal resurrection of the Lord Jesus.

I can discern demons in a number of ways. First, through God's presence that comes upon me, when I stand near to an influenced person. The warm presence of God fills my being in an unusual way. If I then touch the person concerned I can actually feel the snake-like evil, as if I was holding a wriggling serpent. This presence I feel through my hands. Sometimes a person's eyes will reveal a leering gaze of a demon.

An intense brightness of the eyes accompanied with a lustreful look often precedes a demonic manifestation. The possessed individual will often set an hypnotising gaze upon me with uncommonly bright eyes. Sometimes the eyes reveal an awful fear and an indescribable terror. Demons recognise the power of the Holy Ghost resting upon an anointed servant of God. They are desperately afraid of being cast out.

Naming The Spirits

When the Spirit of God is mightily upon me I can actually number and name the demons I am contending with. At times I have cross-questioned these sinister powers, to check the accuracy of my revelation. The revelation is given through the Holy Spirit, and not a product of human imagination. The very nature of a demon is unclean and savours of the pit itself. Often the possessed individual will give off an awful distasteful stench to his breath. It is not just bad breath, it is more powerful than that. Even after the person has vacated the premises the evil odour will still remain.

Sometimes a possessed person becomes agitated and restless in my presence. Their eyes begin to roll and wander. They appear uncomfortable and uneasy and try to avoid my company. This is a certain sign that an evil spirit is at work and has recognised the anointing of God upon me. If I step towards the person concerned the immediate reaction is to cower in fear, or attempt to run away. Sometimes the demons will scream in terror and cast the body they possess to the ground. A person harassed by such an evil influence will resist a physical point of contact. They will often refuse prayer and turn aside suggestions for help and assistance.

Delusion and Fear

Many who are possessed by evil spirits show a great tendency to fear. They refuse to converse and appear afraid and agitated. Others are frequently violent and become uncontrollable and out of hand. Those deluded by false doctrines and teachings often possess an overpowering nature. They repeatedly try to press home their unbalanced teachings. They refuse to partake in an honest discussion, and often with exasperation furnish their doctrines to a stormy climax.

Once again these facts and truths are not the by-product of human imagination. They have to be unearthed and exposed before the remedy is applied. The psychiatrist may delve into the root cause of the problem, but cannot always prescribe a satisfactory solution. God has prescribed a divine remedy. He has made available to the Church gifts and means of discernment, and has empowered His own to deal effectively with these sinister forces.

8

Miracles in Revival

Revival has always been near to my heart. Having been quickened repeatedly by reading the reports of bygone revivals it has been my humble joy and privilege to be a partaker also.

I once preached in the same chapel at Loughor visited by the mighty power of God during the Great Welsh Revival. I handled Evan Robert's famous Bible and ministered in the same pulpit as the renowned revivalist.

During 1971 I witnessed a remarkable move of the Holy Spirit in West Wales.

The nation of Wales once aflame with spiritual blessing has generally turned its back upon God. Church congregations have withered while sin and complacency have blighted the nation. West Wales particularly has been noted for its spiritual indifference. A number of stately churches and places of worship have long struggled to exist with a mere handful of believers. The days of rich spirituality and godliness seemed gone forever.

In the market town of Lampeter, West Wales, however, a local business man, Mr Dan Jones, took the situation to heart. For many years, he and a Christian associate, Mr Gwilym Price, waited before God praying incessantly for a spiritual awakening. When at first nothing transpired they intensified their prayers with occasional fasting.

Undaunted by the lack of local enthusiasm, however, these two local visionaries continued to pray until the floodgates were thrown wide open during the memorable evening of Friday February 26th 1971. God chose for the venue of this re-awakening the Soar Congregational Church, Lampeter. Centrally situated in the market square, this building comfortably accommodates almost eight hundred worshippers. The small town itself boasts a population of about two thousand souls. Following great spiritual blessing in South Wales, I was invited to conduct a special one night meeting in the Soar Chapel.

Despite the hindrances of the postal strike which greatly restricted the advertsing, the resultant interest was so overwhelming that by the commencement of the service the church was filled to capacity. Coaches, cars and vehicles of every description congested the market square, the side streets and avenues. By 7.30 pm every seat in the church was occupied with the residue filling the ante-rooms and overflowing into the vestry. Some were obliged to stand throughout the proceedings. An intense sense of expectancy prevailed. It was obvious to the majority that something remarkable was about to occur.

A Glorious Re-Awakening

The very first meeting of what is now commonly called the West Wales Visitation commenced with the singing of the Welsh hymn. "CYFRIG BENDITHION, UN AC UN," (Count your blessings.) Hundreds of young and old have every reason to count their blessings as a result of this heaven sent re-awakening. By 7.25 pm the convenor Mr Alan Brittain, a local factory manager, introduced the revivalist who delivered to the congregation a ninety minute gospel address. The ministry was convicting and challenging. I spoke of my personal encounters with God and the urgent need for genuine repentance and reconciliation as a prelude to spiritual blessing. I concluded with a soul challenging appeal to all the unconverted present. By this time the awesome presence of God shrouded the attentive congregation. Suddenly a young man seated in the side balcony rose up and with bowed head pushed his way through the crowded aisles to the altar. Upon kneeling at the front he burst into tears and wept profusely. He was followed by a steady stream of seeking souls, some weeping, some solemn faced, melted and broken. It was a most moving response. Soon the front of the church was filled with those seeking the Lord's salvation and forgiveness. The majority knelt spontaneously, buried their heads in their hands and wept freely. The atmosphere was heavily charged with the divine presence. Soon the seekers overflowed into the aisles but due to the congestion were unable to find room to kneel and so remained standing with their heads humbly bowed.

Eventually prayer was offered on their acount. Sinful hearts were instantly transformed. Sorrow and sighing gave way to new found joy and peace.

The converting grace of Jesus flooded many souls. The floodgates were thrown open and the Spirit's power broke forth in torrential blessing. The longed for visitation was underway. I promised prayer for the sick and suffering, and these were called forward in the name of the Lord Jesus.

The Sick Miraculously Blessed

The first to respond was a middle aged lady suffering from a serious internal complaint. But before prayer could be offered she was completely overwhelmed by the power of God. Trembling from head to toe she began praising Jesus for her miraculous release to the astonishment of all present.

Other wonderful incidents followed. A man afflicted with arthritis was so quickened by the Lord's power that he pushed his way up and down the aisle glorifying God. Other arthritics similarly demonstrated their cures. Then the Lord's power fell upon a young man handicapped by a semi paralysed hand which sprang to life at the Master's touch. Excitedly he moved around the congregation, shaking hands with one and another. By this time the majority present were standing upright in order to obtain a better view of the proceedings. A young woman with failing sight shouted with joy, "I can see! Praise God I can see!" Her face shone with joy and surprise. Some standing by burst into tears.

Like Heaven on Earth

Simultaneously the congregation burst into song. Anthem followed anthem until the building vibrated with the praises of the people.

It was like heaven on earth.

By this time the altar was inundated with folk. Many seemed completely overwhelmed with the Holy Spirit.

The meeting continued until 10.40 pm and despite the lateness of the hour the majority were reluctant to leave. When the crowd eventually dispersed one could still hear them singing the praises of the Lord in the streets outside. Small groups remained in the church until well after 11 pm excitedly discussing the events of the evening.

It was obvious to all that God had visited His people but little did one realise that these were the humble beginnings of a far mightier outpouring of the Holy Spirit. Soon the entire population were to be stirred and challenged by the divine events that were to follow.

Following the remarkable revival service on February 26th, I received clear and definite instructions from the Lord to return to the Lampeter locality. The spacious Victoria Hall was hired on this occasion and no less than 4,000 attendances were recorded during the four day revival crusade. At times the vast crowd overflowed in the street outside and scores were obliged to stand throughout the services. Hundreds responded to the call of the gospel and as the news of the re-awakening spread many travelled from far and wide to participate in the visitation.

These heart-stirring events were faithfully reported by the press. One such news report appeared as follows....

A Local Press Report

Is there to be another religious revival in Wales? The Rev. Peter Scothern, the well known evangelist, who paid a return visit to Lampeter last week, said he firmly believed that this revival would start in West Wales.

Rev. Peter Scothern was holding a four-day evangelical crusade at the Victoria Hall, and judging by the attendances there is obviously a thirsting by the populace for religion, and that they are searching for the faith and hope.

On the first evening the hall was packed, and once again the congregation was deeply moved by the speaker's stirring address, and watched with wonderment as many underwent an electrifying experience as the evangelist laid his hands upon them.

Many Turned Away

Each succeeding night the numbers grew, and by Good Friday evening many were turned away because they could not gain admission beyond the foyer, which was crammed with people with eagerly straining eyes and ears to see or hear what was transpiring inside the hall.

Those who had been fortunate enough to get inside saw young and old go forward in search of the blessing of the Lord.

A young boy who was deaf was made to hear. A man who had lost his hearing for fifty years had it restored. Arthritics danced and waved their arms in joy as their stiffness and pain left them.

A Carmarthenshire man, who had hobbled in with the aid of a walking stick, told the evangelist he could now keep the stick as he could now do without it.

Another man who said that he had come to the hall suffering from the pain and discomfort of a stomach ulcer testified that it had cleared after receiving a blessing and went happily to the ante room to enjoy tea and sandwiches.

Another person, who was obviously pleased at the change he felt after Rev. Scothern laid hands on him, was a man who had been suffering from angina and had been warned not to walk quickly or bend down. After walking briskly back and forth and touching his knees, he told his wife: "You needn't tie my shoes any more."

The next night he was back again lustily singing hymns of praise in thanksgiving for his new lease of life.

But he was not the only one to return and give thanks. Several local people who felt benefit from the evangelist's first visit to the town were there assisting in the proceedings and evidently improved in health.

People came from afar, Mr. and Mrs. O. R. Bulkeley, of Kington, Herefordshire, brought along their two daughters Anne and Christine.

Mrs. Bulkeley said that Anne had been a mongol child and was suffering from various complaints before she was taken to Rev. Scothern when seven years old.

"She received a miracle cure through the electrifying power of divine healing, and now, at the age of ten is a normal child. We are a family who just believe with simple faith," she added.

The Unforgettable Good Friday Service

The Good Friday evening service excelled. Early arrivals filled the main hall half an hour before the commencement of the service. The streets and avenues bordering the Victoria hall were lined with vehicles and cars of every description. By 7 pm the crowds overflowed into the annexe and scores were obliged to stand throughout the proceedings. Children surrendered their seats to the adults and gathered themselves at the foot of the platform. Some had travelled over 100 miles to attend the revival. There was an intense sense of expectancy and despite the restlessness due to overcrowding the awe and presence of God was distinctly discerned. At times it seemed as if a glorious haze hung over the congregation. The side doors were eventually opened to allow much needed ventilation.

Scores Overflow Into The Street

The opening Welsh hymn was sung with such fervour that the verses and choruses were frequently repeated. Reports reached the platform that the vast crowd had overflowed into the streets outside while those inside were asked to make more room. The Lord enabled me to deliver a very powerful and most challenging address. God called for genuine repentance and a complete committal to Christ as a prelude to the revival soon to break forth. For nearly an hour and a half the congregation followed each forthright statement with rapt attention and despite the abnormal length of the sermon those present showed no signs of restlessness. As one remarked later, "You could hear a pin drop even after ninety minutes of preaching." The message was climaxed with a fervent appeal to those present to commit themselves to the converting grace of Jesus Christ. Suddenly it seemed as if the entire congregation surged forward in response. The scene was indescribable. Many melted to tears while others sobbed upon the shoulders of their friends. Men and women and children of all ages swept forward until the entire front of the hall and the side aisles were packed with seeking souls. The main hall became a mass of humanity hungering and thirsting after God. Counselling proved impossible and so the visiting pastors and ministers handed out Gospel portions and booklets.

Even Children Healed and Overwhelmed

Prayer and blessing followed for the sick and the suffering. The power of God was so intense that the children around the platform were completely overwhelmed by the Holy Ghost. The sick were instantly blessed the moment they were touched. It was just like a scene from the New Testament. Some struggled through the dense crowd to rush home and bring along their sick friends and neighbours. Such scenes had never been witnessed before in living memory. For days following the Good Friday events in Lampeter were the talk of the community. God had certainly visited the place.

BBC Televises The Lampeter Service

During the Thursday evening of May 13th, BBC Wales televised details of the Lampeter revival services in their programme "Heddiw" at around 7 pm. The review highlighted events during the meeting such as the altar call, testimonies, and the prayer ministry to the sick. The broadcast, however, came a little too late to affect the evening service, nevertheless the Crymmych Market Hall was once again filled to overflowing. In fact it proved necessary to relay the service to those crowded in the rear annexe. About 70 souls stepped forward in response to the Gospel call. It was a most moving spectacle. Young folk wept their way to the Cross, and the majority shed at least a few tears.

The Western Mail Reports

On Tuesday May 11th, the Western Mail faithfully reported the visitation at Lampeter, and dedicated almost half a page of reading matter to the subject. This undoubtedly helped tremendously to inspire interest in Crymmych prior to our arrival. The local shops and stores also participated in the advertsing of the services by displaying posters and window bills. Just as Friday February 26th 1971 had become a memorable day in the hearts of the Lampeter inhabitants, so will Wednesday May 12th 1971 be in the hearts of the residents of Crymmych.

The leaders involved in the Lampeter visitation testified at the conclusion of the first service in Crymmych that this was the most powerful of all services to date. Well over sixty souls surged to the altar to claim the converting grace of Jesus Christ. Some wept profusely as they were led away for counselling. It was an awe inspiring, breathtaking sight. The young were prominent at the altar call. It was a most blessed sight. People of all walks of life flocking to the front of the Market Hall to repent of their sins and lay claim to the saving grace of God. Many prayers were answered that night. The husband of one of the first converts of the revival surrendered to Christ this evening. Many chapel folk were saved. A mother's prayer was answered when her wayward boy was soundly converted. Only eternity will completely reveal all that was wrought this night by the power of God's Spirit.

9

Miracles Among The Children

Christ's compassion and concern for the children is indelibly stamped upon the gospel records. Even when the disciples turned the little ones away Jesus insisted on blessing them.

I have always respected the simple uncomplicated faith of a child. I can pray for them with supreme confidence.

During the remarkable Calcutta Crusade I visited the Circus grounds to check the preparations. While conversing with a company of local ministers we were suddenly confronted by a distressed father carrying a sick child. The little one had been bitten by a scorpion, and was crying bitterly. Her leg was beginning to swell and I will never forget the look of fear in her dark eyes. Taking the child in my arms, I authoritatively commanded the poison to leave her in the Name of Jesus. The Lord's power flowed freely into her little body. Immediately the pain disappeared and within seconds she was smiling with gratitude. I handed her back to her father who bowed gratefully and began giving praise to God. The ministers also joined in the celebration glorifying the name of Jesus.

God's Timing is Perfect

A distressed mother desperately pushed her way to the front of my crowded service. "Are you the Rev. Scothern? My daughter is desperately ill in the local hospital. She has been in a coma for several days in the Intensive Care Unit. Please, please offer a prayer for her tonight."

I assured her that all would be well. So precisely ten minutes to eight I invited the congregation to stand and join hands in compassion and faith for the young girl's restoration. The believing prayers from the assembly were so spontaneous that many promptly burst into praise and thanksgiving anticipating a miracle. The service concluded about 9.30 pm.

As the folks were dispersing the mother of the sick child returned to the meeting. Her face was radiant with joy as she pushed to the front. "Bless God, my daughter is out of her coma. I have been talking to her!" she excitedly proclaimed as she shared the good news with the rest of the congregation.

As an afterthought I publicly enquired of her, "about what time did your daughter make this miraculous recovery?" "At about ten minutes to eight!" she replied. An anthem of praise emanated from the congregation. This was precisely the time that believing prayer had been offered for the sick child. Did not Jesus instruct us to believe our prayers were heard the very moment we pray?

A Miracle in Liverpool

"She can skip now" testified the excited father!

I was crusading in the Wellington Road Baptist Church, Dingle, Liverpool for two unforgettable weeks. Hundreds thronged the place nightly witnessing many dramatic healings, including that of ten year old Marion Kerr. Removing her leg irons her mother watched with tear filled eyes as Marion walked up and down the church aisle strong and well. The local press reporters visited the home of the young miracle child and found Marion skipping outside her home. Her photograph and testimony appeared on the front page of the Liverpool Weekly News.

An Amazing Miracle

Perhaps one of the most amazing miracle healings I have ever witnessed was reported in detail by the BBC in an enthralling documentary entitled "The Kilgetty Healer". This unique programme was shown on the BBC2 network during August 1975. X-Rays were presented on the programme to give indisputable evidence to the reality of the miracle.

"He needs an operation. We'll send for him".

Before these words could sink in, Mr and Mrs King were ushered briskly out of the specialist's consulting room. Stephen, their twenty month old son, was limping beside them.

It was in June 1970 that the orthopaedic specialist

studied Stephen's X-Ray. He declared that there was no hip socket on the right side necessitating an early operation. There was no bone where there should have been and there was bone where there should not have been. The hip joint was completely dislocated and one leg was shorter than the other. A major operation was needed.

Mr. and Mrs. King asked for a second opinion and visited an eminent orthopaedic specialist in Birmingham. A further X-Ray was taken. After studying it the specialist said, "I'm sorry, I have to agree that Stephen urgently requires an operation on the right hip and there is no other solution. Without it Stephen will be permanently crippled."

Being a State Registered Nurse Mrs. King knew what the operation would entail. It would mean weeks or maybe months in plaster of paris. Furthermore, she was certain that the hospitalisation of Stephen would cause serious emotional problems, as several enforced separations during babyhood had already affected him.

As a mother she was very sad and burdened, but how precious it is during such times to know the friendship of Jesus. Mr. and Mrs. King simply handed their problem over to the Lord.

The Healing Revelation

At this point God revealed to Stephen's mother something she had never previously realised. Their

Bible reading the following morning centred around the eighth chapter of Matthew. The Holy Spirit illuminated verse seventeen in a new and living way:- "(JESUS) Himself took our infirmities and bare our sicknesses."

They had previously acknowledged that Jesus had borne their sins on the Cross, but now saw clearly that He also bore their *sickness*. They further rejoiced in verse sixteen where it faithfully declares that Jesus healed *all* that were sick. Also they claimed the promise, "Jesus Christ the SAME yesterday and today and forever." (Heb. 13:8).

Mr. and Mrs. King explained to their specialist how they felt concerning faith in God's Word. He replied, "Faith is alright in its place, but this is not just a question of healing. Your son needs a complete reconstruction of the hip joint and this can only be accomplished by a surgical operation."

Faithfully supported by the prayers of Christian friends Stephen's parents held fast to the promises of God. For a while Stephen continued to limp badly and could not walk without falling. Then through a remarkable series of circumstances they were introduced to my God-given ministry. They promptly wrote to me requesting prayer and I mailed a faith-inspiring letter along with an anointed prayer cloth. (Acts 19:11-12).

That night, while Stephen slept, Mrs. King laid the prayer cloth over his right hip, in the Name of Jesus, asking God to work a creative miracle. Although Stephen was lying perfectly still, Mrs. King felt movements in the hip beneath her hand.

Within moments God created a new bone and miraculously performed the reconstruction. The following morning Stephen was able to jump, skip, climb and even kick a football. He kept running up and down the fifty foot long drive without falling.

During August Stephen's parents returned to visit the orthopaedic specialist and a new X-Ray was taken. He studied it very carefully and then compared it with the previous X-Rays. He then informed Mr. and Mrs. King *that both hips* were normal and the pending operation was unnecessary. The final X-Ray proved scientifically that God's power had touched Stephen, making him whole. Stephen later invited Christ into his heart. All praise and glory be to God.

Excema Vanishes in Jesus Name

Billy had suffered with excema since he was a baby in arms. He was nearly eight years of age when he attended my healing service in South Yorkshire. I distinctly remember Billy rolling up his coat sleeve and saying "Can God cure this?"

"Yes Billy, if you trust Him with all your heart and serve Him with all your strength" I replied. "That's great", said Billy and I promptly anointed him with oil in the Name of Jesus.

The following month I returned to the same Baptist Church. Billy was there waiting on the steps of the chapel. His face was beaming with delight. I was greeted with "He's done it! He's done it!" Sure enough Billy's arms were completely clear of excema. God had removed every trace. Billy gave testimony to a packed and praising congregation that same evening.

Gipsy Boy Jason Receives Healing

I was ministering in a West Wales Baptist Church and the congregation included a company of gipsy folk. Young Jason Roberts suffered a serious heart defect. His mother presented him to the Lord when I requested the sick and suffering to come forward. Jason observed the proceedings with rapt attention and showed no sign of shyness! Laying my hands upon him in the Lord's Name I distinctly experienced God's power surging through me. I **knew** Jason was healed. Turning to his mother I said "God has healed your son. Follow after the Lord and serve Him faithfully."

Having set Jason down on the floor I instructed him to run up and down the aisle. Without hesitation the young gipsy boy raced around the chapel, and returned to the front. Showing no sign of his heart complaint, his mother lifted up her hands and gave praise to God. Jason later attended a Cardiff Hospital where he was informed that his heart was sound and normal.

"Jesus Miraculously Healed My Son of a Hole in the Heart"

The Personal Testimony of Mrs. Roberts.
"Jason was born in Pembroke, West Wales during 1972. From the very tender age of ten days we discovered that he was suffering from a hole in the heart. He was a very weak and sickly child, always attending the hospital. We were very anxious and concerned about his future.

When Jason was two years old we heard that healing Evenagelist Peter Scothern was holding a special healing service at the Baptist Church Pembroke. We attended the service taking Jason with us. At the invitation we went forward and brother Peter laid hands upon our little son in the Name of Jesus. God's servant prayed very positively and we put our trust in the Lord.

From that time Jason grew up and began running around, kicking a football and doing everything a normal boy would do. He has never once complained of his heart and has always been healthy and well.

Eight months ago we attended the hospital at Cardiff and subsequent tests have proved a pending operation is not necessary, and that Jason's heart is completely healed.

Every time brother Peter ministers in the area, we take Jason along to testify. Last week, he ran up and down the aisle of the Baptist Church to show the congregation that the Lord had miraculously healed him."

Andrew Received Supernatural Hair

Young Andrew was born *without any hair cells in his body*. By the time he was eight years old his condition became most embarrassing. Some of Europe's leading specialists confirmed that his problem was incurable.

Returning home from school one day, he received a handbill advertising our Divine Healing Services in the village of Summerhill. His grandmother agreed to accompany him. Young Andrew listened intently to the Gospel message and was fully persuaded that Jesus would heal him.

Andrew presented himself for the laying on of hands, and returned home full of expectancy. Every morning afterwards he would say to his parents, "Look and see if my hair is growing." Andrew never once doubted the Lord would heal him. Some eight weeks later he experienced the first signs of new growth on his head. Slowly but progressively Andrew's hair grew. He thanked God each day for his miracle – exactly as I had instructed him. Eventually the young boy was blessed with normal natural hair. One evening Andrew again joined the healing line.

"Why have you come for prayer again", I asked him.

"Uncle Peter" he replied, "my hair is growing curly like a little girl's, and I want it to grow straight!" Believe it or not, God answered this prayer also.

Everyone was so excited and gave glory to God. This testimony provided by Jason's parents Mr. and Mrs. Roberts, of Pembroke, Dyfed, West Wales.

Totally Deaf Ears Opened

Maria was six years old when I visited Abeokuta, Nigeria for the memorable West African Crusade.

The local Chief allowed me the use of the palace grounds. I can recall a dozen prisoners hauling large pieces of timber to construct the platform. There was a tremendous interest in the Crusade. The very first evening some two thousand inhabitants gathered to hear the gospel and witness the mighty works of God.

As I stepped onto the platform someone lifted a child into my arms. It was little Maria. I will never forget her beautiful eyes and rich, dark skin. I enquired as to why I was handed the little girl. A local man replied in broken English "She cannot hear! She is deaf."

The eyes of all present were centred upon the platform. I took Maria in my arms and prayed compassionately for Jesus to heal her for the glory of God. At first nothing happened, so I prayed a second time, commanding Maria's ears to be opened in the Name of Jesus. As soon as I removed my hands her face radiated with assurance. First I clapped my hands quietly and she nodded approval. I repeated the action more loudly and she promptly put her hands over her ears. The noise was too intense for

Maria's deaf ears had miraculously opened. I then proceeded with two syllable words "MAMMA – DADDA." Maria spoke her first words. Suddenly the congregation erupted with shouts of praise.

Within seconds a score or more little children were being pushed onto the platform to be blessed. *So* many children needed divine healing.

The following day when I visited Maria at her home to take her details and photographs, I discovered she was beginning to speak additional words. The entire population attended the Crusade to hear the glorious Gospel of Jesus Christ and to witness God confirming His Word with signs following.

Blind Sierra Leone Girl Instantly Healed

I was crusading for Christ in Freetown, Sierra Leone during 1985. Thousands attended services in the Central Park.

One evening a young girl, blind in both eyes, suddenly received her sight. She cried out with joy "God made me see! God made me see!"

I promptly jumped down from the platform, while the crowd pushed the young girl to the front. Sure enough the young girl could see everything and excitedly pointed in every direction. I lifted her onto the platform for everyone to see as she demonstrated her new sight. A great shout of praise to God resounded through the multitude.

Incredible Miracle in the U.S.A.

During my first visit to the United States I was introduced to Ronald Coyne. He was blind in one eye, and wore an artificial eye. His testimony was almost unbelievable.

One day Ronald went forward to receive divine healing. Upon receiving the laying on of hands, he experienced a brilliant light in his blind eye. From that moment Ronald Coyne could see perfectly through his artificial eye. This phenomena astounded everybody. Even I found it hard to believe, but when I personally tested his sight I was obliged to acknowledge that Ronald Coyne could see perfectly through an "artificial eye!" *"Is there ANYTHING too hard for the LORD?"* (Genesis 18:14).

Making the Dumb to Speak

During one of my memorable gospel crusades in Freetown, Sierra Leone, thousands gathered in the central public park. Many sick and afflicted attended those great open air services. They would arrive hours before the start and sit patiently under large black umbrellas to protect themselves from the burning sun.

One evening after the service commenced a charabang of young children arrived. Their ages ranged from five to twelve years. They all shared a common ailment – they were deaf and dumb. The stewards guided them to the front of the vast congregation.

I was directed by the Lord to invite the local clergy, priests and deacons to come forward and stand with the children. Each minister was requested to select a child and lay hands over their ears in the all powerful Name of Jesus.

A holy hush fell upon the congregation. The Lord enabled me to pray with great power and authority.

"Lord Jesus, glorify your name and show forth your omnipotent power and boundless compassion – show these people that you *are* the living Lord, and Creator of all things. Command the opening of every deaf ear and the loosing of every dumb tongue – among these little children for your praise and glory."

Suddenly the Holy Spirit descended upon the ministers and the children. Remarkably the first miracle which occurred was the instant healing of a blind ten year old. The young girl suddenly cried out that she could see the lights and the faces of the folk around her. This spontaneous divine happening electrified the proceedings.

The ministers quickly discovered that some of the deaf children were beginning to hear clearly and distinctly. There was tremendous excitement as one by one the children were lifted to the platform. Speaking directly into their little ears, I would use words like "MAMMA," "DADDA," "JESUS."

You can imagine the intense excitement when it became increasingly clear that the children could speak and hear. Twenty two youngsters were carefully tested and only two failed the test. We prayed a second time for these.

Afterwards I used short sentences and other words which were quickly repeated. Some of the parents were weeping for joy, hugging their children and giving praise and glory to God. Those present will never forget the radiant faces of those West African children whose deaf ears were opened and dumb tongues were loosed by the wonderful power of God.

"And with great power gave the apostles witness of the resurrection of the Lord Jesus: and great grace was upon them all."

(Acts 4:33)

"But ye shall receive power, after that the Holy Ghost is come upon you: and ye shall be witnesses unto Me both in Jerusalem, and in all Judea, and in Samaria, and unto the uttermost part of the earth."

(Acts 1:8)

The Wonderful Healing of Michael Barnes

Occupying the front cover of one of my 'Deliverance' magazines is the photograph of nine years old Michael Barnes.

It was during the Seacroft Crusade in the United Reformed Church that God bestowed upon Michael his special miracle.

Started Limping

The first sign Michael detected of his illness was a stiffening of the knee. As this condition intensified he started limping badly. This was followed by a high temperature which resulted in a visit to the Leeds dispensary. After careful examination Michael was immediately admitted to the James Hospital. For four weeks he was subjected to observations and tests, and eventually transferred to a children's hospital.

The specialist in charge of this case gave no hope of immediate recovery, and told Mrs. Barnes that it would be a prolonged illness. Michael's legs were scheduled to be in plaster for many wearying months. Receiving this disheartening news Mrs. Barnes attended my Deliverance and Healing Crusade. Special prayer was offered for Michael, and a handkerchief prayed over in accordance with Acts 19:11-12. This was taken to the children's hospital, and placed over Michael's legs, with the nurses prayerfully co-operating.

Amazing Recovery

Within days Michael made a most remarkable recovery. He was soon discharged from the hospital completely cured. Within two weeks he was home again enjoying a normal life. Every trace of Osteo Myalitis disappeared. Michael Barnes is now a teenager, and remains fit and well. He can run and jump without weakness or pain. For many years he has proved the goodness of God. This young lad was destined to months of suffering but God's power met his great need.

What the Lord has wrought in the life of Michael Barnes HE IS WILLING TO DO FOR ANY CHILD WHO WILL TRUST AND OBEY HIM.

Jesus said,

> *"Suffer the little children to come unto Me, and forbid them not, for such is the Kingdom of God. Verily I say unto you, whosoever shall not receive the Kingdom of God as a little child, shall not enter therein. And He took them up in His arms, put His hands upon, and blessed them."*

(Mark 10:14-15)

Peter Scothern would welcome your genuine enquiries and prayer requests.
Please write to:
Divine Healing Ministries,
P.O. Box 61,
Gloucester GL2 6UT
England.